Philip Jerome Cleveland

It's

BRIGHT

in My

VALLEY

FLEMING H. REVELL COMPANY

Library of Congress Catalog Card Number: 62-10734

Printed in the United States of America

1.1

Part of the chapter "New-Mown Hay and Healing" was published in *The Church in the Home,* January-March, 1954, under the title of "Out in the Field with God"; "The Magic Road to Anywhere" also appeared as "How We Started a Church School" in the July-September, 1959 issue of the same publication. Both are reprinted by permission.

The following have appeared in *Church Management* and are reprinted by permission: "My Friend Jim" appeared in the December, 1960 issue as "Derelict in the Dark"; "The Word That Came Alive," February, 1961; "Sunrise for a Doctor"; "A Wedding Gown for Mazie" appeared as "Salt Water, the Wayward and a Wedding"; "A Believer in Karl Marx" appeared under the title "Commies, Crisis and the Church"; also, "A Russian, a Reason and a Recruit."

The "plant a chair" incident in "Irish Cobblers and the Inevitable" was published as an article in "Life in These United States" in *The Reader's* Digest for August, 1945. Other material incorporated in this chapter was published in *The New England Homestead.* These are reprinted by permission.

The poem "The Builder" was first published in *Christian Herald,* copyright by *Christian Herald* and used by special permission. The chapter "Portrait of a Mother" appeared in the September, 1950 issue under the title of "Story of Love" and is reprinted by permission.

To
FULTON OURSLER
counselor, critic, comrade

FOREWORD

This book beats time to the old tune that truth is stranger than fiction. It is a song book about valleys, particularly the multi-colored, river-veined Quinebaug Valley in northeastern Connecticut. From these pool-green pastures, church spires thrust white fingers of blessing to God.

Each chapter is a sincere record of strange, amusing, often dramatic experience. Each chapter delineates a moment in a rural pastor's day. Indians knew these haunts which throbbed with drama, love, beauty, long before white men, centuries before a venturesome preacher decided to explore their highlights and shadows.

"Darker grows the valley," mused George Meredith in a trying, lonely hour. For my part I must confess that I found my valley becoming the proverbial path of the just, a shining light, shining more and more into perfect day. Canterbury was and is a little place, even as Windham County and the robin-tuned, maple-sweet valley of the Quinebaug where for many years I preached. I also published and edited a weekly newspaper, *The Quinebaug Valley News.*

I have recorded "my little system," remembering the lines of an exceedingly wise man:

Our little systems have their day;
They have their day and cease to be;
They are but broken lights of thee,
And thou, O Lord, art more than they.
—Alfred Tennyson

Philip Jerome Cleveland
The First Congregational Church
New Bedford, Massachusetts

CONTENTS

A Wedding Gown for Mazie

A PRIM, EFFICIENT church organist lived on a rocky island off the stern coast of Maine. As her pastor, I was boarding with her and her genial husband.

The little fishing community of lobster traps, salty lines and damaged anchors faced a romantic crisis. I became aware of it when my host remarked to his wife at supper, "Mazie would like to get married—and can't."

"And why not?" replied the organist.

"She says she won't get married until she gets a wedding dress. Jim can't afford one, the fishing season being what it is."

"What is that to me?" retorted his wife, a bit sharply.

"Wasn't she in your Sunday school class once? Didn't you try hard to make something out of Mazie?"

"Nobody can do anything with the girl!" the young woman judged with the chill voice of an off-shore wind.

When her husband had gone to do some late chores, the wife spoke to me in exasperation.

9

"Mazie never had a proper bringing up! We all tried to appeal to her, to mend her ways. We tried to challenge her to better things. She abandoned the Sunday school, stopped attending church and the youth services. Her language is careless, she scorns decent society and it might be a blessing if she quit the village altogether!"

I did not think it wise to say much. However, I did remark that one must be kind to the poor, to those who had been deprived of a prayerful home life. "Perhaps married life is the answer," I suggested. "Jim is a good worker."

"He's as poor as Job's turkey!" she blurted. "How can he afford a decent wedding and all the fixings?" She glared at me. I turned to make a quiet, pastoral withdrawal.

"He can't!" With this edict she lifted the supper plates from the table and vanished into the kitchen.

Late that night I heard the husband and wife discussing Mazie's problem. "You have your wedding dress," he boomed. "You have it up in the attic trunk. Mazie is just about your size."

"What on earth are you saying?" Her voice was raised in petulance and anger. A door slammed and silence returned to the house sheltered by shore pines. For two weeks one could feel the tense, thunder-filled air in their home as well as throughout the village.

One afternoon I was reading the Bible in my upstairs study when I heard my door creak. My hostess, dressed

in shining white, entered and stood in the sunlight stream-
ing through a window facing the sea.

"Do you like it?" she asked. "I wore it six years ago,
and it still fits!" Gaily she laughed as she curtsied. "I love
it so! And my husband wants me to give it away—to that
poor, simple Mazie. Just think!" She whirled, almost
fiercely. "My wedding gown!"

I said nothing. I lifted the Book I was reading and
showed her one well-thumbed page: ". . . whatsoever ye
would that men should do to you, do ye even so to
them . . ." (Matthew 7:12).

Her blue eyes scanned the sun-haloed sentence; a flush
of crimson crossed her handsome face. "Well, you may
believe that, but I don't!" she snapped as she left the
room, slamming the door.

The silent drama of discouraged Jim, melancholy
Mazie, and a postponed wedding came to a climax one
unforgettable Friday night a few weeks later.

It was almost time for the little weekly prayer meeting, which the organist usually attended. My host was
called to a fishermen's gathering, and the moment he left
the front porch I saw his wife scurry upstairs. Twenty
minutes later she knocked on my study door and brought
in a large parcel, beautifully wrapped.

"Pastor, I have made my decision." She held a hand-
kerchief to her eyes. "On the way to the prayer meeting,
will you kindly drop around to Mazie's house and leave
this? Just leave it—without one word. Don't breathe a

word of this to a living soul, please. I slipped a little card inside: 'From a Friend.' Will you do that for me?"

"You aren't coming to the meeting tonight?"

"Oh, not tonight," she said faintly as she looked away.

I did exactly as she requested. In the darkness I placed the parcel in front of a humble door, rang the bell and, for once in my life, ran away.

One month later Jim and Mazie were pronounced man and wife before a sacred altar in the beautifully decorated church fronting the bracing Atlantic.

The organist played the wedding march as Jim and Mazie walked up the aisle; and of that hour she spoke later, laughing and crying at the same time, and with a bright courage shining in her eyes. "You know, Pastor, it was just like being married all over again."

The Cruise of
the *Bear River*

I WAS FISHING for a ship's cook, trying to get him seated
at the Lord's table. His wife and children urged me to
keep after Hazeltine; I would land him yet. Whenever
the *Bear River* lay at dock I never saw him; he was for-
ever somewhere else. It became evident that I must go
to sea to net him for a quiet chat.

For some months I had observed the picturesque little
packet steamer moving up and down the narrow, twisting river. It docked at the wharf of Clarke and Cunning-
ham. The *Bear River* shuttled back and forth across the
Bay of Fundy, from Digby, Nova Scotia, to St. John,
New Brunswick, challenging one of the roughest bodies
of water, with the highest tides, in the world.

Captain John Woodworth, expert old sea dog, leader
in the Tabernacle Church at the head of the tide in the
village, was famous in the provinces for his seamanship.
He, too, was anxious to get his elusive cook, Hazeltine,
to church. I mentioned my plans to the captain.

"Good! Take a trip with us. It's the only way you'll ever grapple him. Throw the anchor right on him. And do you know that the preacher you are always talking about, the Reverend Mr. Morgan, will be holding a week's meetings in St. John next month?"

"Dr. G. Campbell Morgan of London?"

"The very man! He'll be at the Methodist Tercentenary Church for a week. We can lay over an extra day or two, and you can attend the special meetings."

"Wonderful!"

A month later I stood on the deck of the *Bear River* as she slowly poked her blunt, gray nose seaward. The voyage across the bay, forty rough miles, was not particularly exciting. My bed in the steaming boiler room was insufferable, so the captain offered me his bunk. "Thank you so much," I said, grateful for the thoughtfulness of this white-bearded man who resembled an ancient patriarch.

However, all through the night, I seemed to be seeking not an elusive, flesh-and-blood Hazeltine, but determined and invisible enemies. My neck grew hot, feverish. When I prepared to shave in the morning and stood before a cracked mirror, I saw that my face was covered with bites, sores and perforations. What a sight I was for a visit ashore!

Carm and Peck, the first and second mates, laughed; the deck hands laughed, and the cook crawled out of his galley to howl. Even the stern captain laughed.

"Didn't know we had such prime livestock aboard the old tub!" the cook shouted. "Heh, lads, the captain's holdin' out on us. Takes the preacher to *find things out*." I still shudder, recalling that night's encounter. Back to the sputtering boiler room I hastened.

When we reached St. John, I discovered how lonely a young minister can be in a great city. My family was in distant Massachusetts, and a forty-mile sea lane separated me from a girl I had come to love. Into my unforgettable homesickness came the tremendous impact of Dr. G. Campbell Morgan.

For three nights I listened spellbound to the gaunt, leather-faced Englishman, his thin neck engulfed in a high clerical collar—a white-haired man of most distinguished bearing. When he preached, his face glowed and I have never since heard such profound, inspired words. I was determined to shake hands with this man of God who was bringing us the good news from a far country.

Each night I studied the lay of the land. I noticed that Dr. Morgan always departed on the left of the pulpit, passing through a short corridor into the distant shadows.

The instant the benediction was pronounced on my last evening in St. John, I ran down the side aisle, which was beginning to fill with people, to the pulpit, then into the corridor and took my station.

Eternity seemed to pass before a tall, thin frame

loomed in the corridor—alone. The easy-swinging form moved my way. For a moment I wavered, then thrust forth a hand.

"Dr. Morgan, I would like to shake hands with you."

He grasped my hand, a curious expression on his gray-tan face, as though he were amazed to find a raw, callow but eager youth in the dim corridor. Suddenly the meditative eyes smiled, he shook my hand fervently and went on his way. I can still feel the warmth of that sincere handshake and have since believed that the fervent handshake of a righteous man availeth much.

In an hour I was back upon the grimy deck of the *Bear River,* waiting for the precise tide upon which to challenge once again the Bay of Fundy and the entrance to Digby Gut. Captain Woodworth was staring at the glass and scanning his watch.

"We've got to make this tide," he said, "but I don't like the looks of that glass. It's likely to be a dirty crossing."

At 1:45 A.M. smoke whirred from the throbbing stack, a lusty whistle penetrated the fog-bound harbor and despite a threatening storm and a huge Boston liner somewhere in the Bay, the game little steamer lumbered off into the darkness.

Said Peck to the captain: "The *Prince George* is out there somewhere."

"We've got to make this tide."

Said Carm: "We got a heap o' cargo."

16

"We've got to beat the storm. Look at that falling glass!"

"It's as black as pitch," chattered Hazeltine.

"We'll make a run for the Gut!" The captain said adamantly.

Will I ever forget the forty miles to the Gut? In the thundering, foggy space the steamer was nothing more than a daub of gray upon the ocean. Staggering up the black steeps, she would rear and plunge into some yawning grave and wallow there, weak, gasping for breath.

Again and again the ship shook under the furious impact of the waves, her shattered strength, shuddered in the maw of the sea, black smoke staggering from the stack, engines shaking the hull. Then, pulsating with fierce, desperate life the determined ship would commence another writhing ascent only to plunge again into a brackish crater.

"We'll never make it!" Carm cried to the frightened cook. "Never! The old tub can't take a beatin' like this!" Hazeltine shivered as a tremendous wave splintered along the starboard rail. Captain Woodworth's fingers were like ice on the wheel. Peck lashed himself to the windlass pole and strained his eyes into the howling darkness.

"You sure, Cap'n, we can run 'er through tonight?" Peck stammered.

"We can't turn back in a sea like this! We'd capsize—you know that."

On through the fearful night the little steamer fought

17

its stubborn, defiant way, at times wallowing until the crew swore the end had come. Hazeltine stumbled into the galley, prepared for the inevitable. He scratched a few lines in the back of an old book he rummaged from his bunk, and said he felt sad about leaving his wife and children. What would become of them?

In that fateful hour I had my few words with the frightened cook. He found time then to talk about God, the seas of life, the great Captain of the Sea of Galilee. He let me pray for him. I hesitate to record my own fears as I thought about a distant Massachusetts slope and a girl.

A short time later, the captain said, "Must be getting nearly across. Must be near the Gut."

Waves were less violent. The captain signaled to reduce speed. Bells sounded in the engine room. Captain Woodworth thrust his hardy face through the open window of the pilot house, out into the clouds of cold, salt fog swirling by. The ship rose and fell across the waters, phosphorescent at the stern, like some phantom of the mist desolately alone on an impenetrable sea. The only ocean discernible was whirling in black circles beside the ship. A bell clanked dull and dead out of the fog leeward; a dim strip of red trembled for an instant in the darkness.

"What is that, mate?" called the captain, straining his dripping face toward the motionless man lashed to the windlass pole.

18

"Buoy No. Five."

Again the captain called: "What is that bell to starboard?"

"Another buoy."

"Which one?"

"Can't make out."

"Where's the light from No. Three?"

"Thought I got it a moment ago—to port."

"Then where's that fog signal from the light?"

"Don't know. Puzzles me. Mebbe the wind's too strong, breezin' up. Can't understand it. Should hear it. Mighty near the Gut now. Takin' account o' wind and tide, displacement and slack, we should be at the entrance any minute."

The captain again signaled the engine room for reduced speed and the boat wriggled slowly, uncertainly, through the crumbling waves. Now we faced something more deadly than waves, wind or fog—the invincible bluffs guarding each side of the Gut.

The entrance to Digby Harbor, Nova Scotia, is the nightmare of all sea captains. It is one of the most hazardous in creation with a hidden, treacherous channel, lined with jagged ledges, its bottom covered with a decaying stratum of perished ships.

"Do you see anything, mate?"

"Not a thing, sir."

"Do you hear anything?"

"Not a thing, sir."

As the tiny packet steamer slowly struggled on, Carm and Hazeltine braced for the shock of wreckage, the grinding of cruel rocks against the old hull. And then the vessel sailed, a boat-length, clean out of the fog, and myriad misty lights flickered ahead. The men were speechless.

Ahead were the lanterns of Digby—the harbor sought and won. The delicately illumined waters of the bay tumbled musically. Beside the *Bear River*, to starboard, rose the bulk of the nearest bluff, not a quarter of a mile away. Behind us coiled the fog, like a long, gray, sea serpent brooding over the dark chaos.

Carm scratched his few strands of iron-gray hair in sheer amazement. Peck declared it was a masterpiece "o' dead reckonin'." Hazeltine rushed to the galley and tore up his farewell words to his good wife. As for me, well, I was beginning to think of next Sunday's sermon. It would certainly be a fit one for any seaman's bethel.

That afternoon the brave little steamer released another sudden, hoarse blast about one half mile above the village. A tired, battered, but happy *Bear River* nosed between the green hills and rested beside the wharf.

Peck said he would never forget a tribute to Captain Woodworth from a retired seaman who had guided one of the great luxury liners that joined New York City to Southampton, England. "Ye gods and little fishes!" the old man had exclaimed. "The captain fetched her across last night! It just can't be! Why, he went and fetched that old tub across in that storm!"

When Carm tossed the grimy lines to the men waiting at the wharf I was already halfway to land. I seemed to roll and wallow for the next week.

Best of all, a shy, silent Hazeltine rolled his way into the snug harbor of a church pew for the first time in his life. He liked the feel of the place and decided to cast anchor there. Often on a prayer meeting night, he would call for his favorite hymn:

> I've anchored my soul in the haven of rest,
> I'll sail the wide seas no more;
> The tempest may sweep o'er the wild, stormy deep,
> In Jesus I'm safe evermore.

Under the Yoke

I HAVE A SERIES of Port Clyde, Maine, paintings and a photo of the trim little church where it all happened. No one there today knows about the struggle of a lonely preacher who walked the rocky shores, the sun-bleached wharves, and the winding roads, with crayons and sketchbook. No one knows about the sudden appearance of a white sail on the horizon, the meeting of a minister and a scholarly stranger.

We met in an almost empty railroad coach along the shores of the Pine Tree State. He sat behind me. There were only four of us in the car.

"You are a stranger in these parts, are you not?" he inquired, tapping my shoulder.

"Yes. I'm preaching at the little church down the road for the next three Sundays."

"A preacher. Well, well. Aren't you a mite young for the trade?"

He was perhaps forty years old, with dark hair, lively black eyes, thin, classic lips curved in an earnest, kind expression which was emphasized by an immaculate moustache. His voice was gentle but firm.

"I am a scholar, a lecturer in southern colleges," he explained. "I have quite a few books to my credit. Now I'm collecting data for a new volume. My life, so far, has been spent with young people. I am very fond of them. Tell me—how did a bright lad like you ever get snared into the church?"

He listened politely, with an amused smile, as I told him about my decision to enter the Christian ministry when I was attending the Metropolitan Museum of Fine Arts School in Boston.

"And you—deserted art—for the pulpit? You gave up the beautiful world of aesthetics for grim, drab ethics? That is hard to believe. Why did you make such a choice?"

"I had to."

"You had to?"

"Yes, I was under the yoke."

"Under what yoke?"

"The yoke of Christ. He fairly drove me into the ministry."

"You mean that a Palestinian Jew, dead two thousand years, buried on a lost hill, drove you into a church? You have an intelligent face. Certainly you are not *serious*."

"But I am."

"You mean a Palestinian Jew became a real, psychological force in your life? It was your father, your mother—they urged you into the church."

"They had tried, but they failed. The Palestinian Jew, as you say, became more living, more real than anyone. I shall never forget the hour—I was only sixteen—when His voice thundered in my soul."

"Illusion, hallucination!" he exclaimed. "It was subjective, unsound! The subliminal consciousness fooled you, young man."

"His voice is still the most powerful, dynamic thing I have ever experienced, sir."

We were at journey's end in a few minutes. The stranger bade me a curious farewell and said he hoped I would enjoy my few days at Port Clyde. Church friends greeted me and when I looked about for him— he was gone.

Imagine my surprise when, five minutes after the Sunday service began, the scholar, faultlessly attired, slipped into a rear pew. After service he approached me.

"Where do you go for dinner?"

"Haven't been invited yet."

"You are invited now. How about a chicken dinner on my yacht? I have a cook who can't be equaled."

He rowed me in a skiff to a handsome yacht, introduced me to the colored skipper and the colored cook. Before dinner we sat in the elegant lounge while my host criticized William Jennings Bryan.

"Bryan is a quitter!" he said sharply. "When he was Secretary of State he quit Woodrow Wilson—during a war. Are Christians quitters? Bryan was a great Bible man, but he was a bigot. He fought science, knowledge, human progress."

"I do not believe he did. It is hard at times to reconcile threatening events with the ethics of the Nazarene."

A certain wistfulness clothed his face like a dawn mist as he asked, "Do you really believe in this Palestinian?"

"He is the one real fact in my life."

After moments of profound silence he thrust more questions before me. "You really think that the ethics of this Palestinian Jew are sound for the twentieth century? Do you believe that Almighty God can be real to people, as real to other people as He is to you?"

During dinner, as the lecturer replenished my plate and issued orders to the cook, he said, "Have you closely observed the cook?"

"Somewhat, yes."

"He has been with me for years. He will work until he has a pocket filled with money. Then he slips away and finds comrades, drinks, squanders his money on loose women."

"Then he is immoral!"

"No, he is not."

"Then what is he?"

"He is *unmoral*. I have tried to teach him moral values. He doesn't see the difference between good and bad, right and wrong. He is unmoral."

We talked on a sunny wharf one bright day; we talked on a rock-strewn shore another day. There was a second

Sunday service, a second invitation to the graceful ship, another long dialogue before and during a luscious dinner.

Once, for an instant, he drew back the curtains that hid the deep places of a proud man's soul. "I had a beautiful wife, Pastor. She was everything that I had dared believe she was. I had her for four wonderful years. Then she became incurably ill. I spent a fortune on her, but nothing could help. She died. That was the only time in my life I prayed. I prayed, if ever a man prayed. And what good did it do? Nobody heard me!" The storm ceased as suddenly as it commenced.

How difficult it is for a pastor to cure souls as sick and hurt as his! I was very young and I extended what words I had. My heart ached for him—and for my own bleak impotence. I knew that the prolonged sea voyages, the thronged classrooms, the elegant dinners had not healed him. Nor could I!

"Oh, Pastor," he confessed, "I pose as a man of science, philosophy, psychology. But if I could believe in a future life, in a good God, and if I could just have her again, I would trade my immense library, my yacht, my mansion—everything—for this knowledge! If I could actually *believe* that your crucified Palestinian Jew spoke timeless truth! Excuse me. I'm sorry I let myself go. I am a bit overemotional—at times. Please let me row you ashore."

He did not speak another word to me. In silence he

waved farewell. And late that very afternoon, I watched from a shore window as the white sails of his yacht filled with new-risen wind and slid across a far, lavender horizon. I felt, that moment, as lonely on the rocky shore as though the world had become suddenly uninhabited.

The next day I sauntered to the wharf where the skiff was tied. I was standing among fishermen, nets, cordage, anchors, pierheads, lobster traps, fishing boats. I have always wondered whether I caught—with the miraculous gospel net properly flung—a rare fish cast up to my feet by the illimitable tides. I was so very young and inexperienced and I hardly knew how to go about my business. Most sincerely do I hope and pray that in that strange, solemn hour I had, by grace of God, what wise men still call "fishermen's luck."

Second Honeymoon

ONE RADIANT MAY morning a man driving a bus east and a pastor driving his car west met in the congested shopping center of Willimantic. I have had many a jolly ride in the Connecticut Company buses, but on this particular Tuesday morning I clambered aboard one and didn't ride! I went nowhere and yet within fifteen minutes I seemed to be traveling at breakneck speed and a marriage I had solemnized began spinning in front of my eyes.

Harry drove for the Connecticut Company, and as his bus stopped at the station and spilled a handful of passengers he saw me passing. I was preoccupied with business.

"Hey, Pastor!" he called, his voice penetrating the infernal clatter of shopping day. "I got to see you. *Today!* It's important. I'll be at the railroad station in ten minutes. Got a fifteen-minute stop there." He closed the thick door and the bus lumbered along.

Ten minutes later I found the bus parked in the sun. Harry opened the big door for me.

"Glad there are no passengers yet!" he blurted. "Sure

glad I ran into you. I was coming to your house. Laura left me, bag and baggage. She won't come back. It's been three weeks now and things at home are one big mess!" His eyes appealed to me, his lively hands as well.

Harry's people were English, and his wife was a wholesome, individualistic "swamp Yankee." Four years ago I had married them and a gala day it had been.

Laura, twenty-three, had really fallen for Harry, who was then a widower of thirty-eight with four sons and a grandfather in his home. People had criticized Laura for taking a chance on love under such challenging conditions. Some had praised her for revealing the pioneer courage rumored to have been in her family. A little girl of two-and-one-half years had graced Harry's second marriage.

"She's taken the girl and gone, perhaps for good!" Harry, usually shy, was now at no loss for words.

"Well, a lover's quarrel," I said, "a spat. She'll get over it. Laura is hot-tempered, but solid to the core. There's always a first time for everything, they say."

"But it's not the first time!" he exploded. "It's the third time and somehow it seems different."

"Where is she?"

"With her parents."

"They want to separate you?"

"Maybe not, but they didn't send her back, either."

"Tell me what happened."

"She says I'm not sympathetic, cooperative—I'm selfish, I exist only for money. She says I'm not the sort to marry. Boy! Oh, boy! She really gave me a rough going over. What'll I do?"

"Let us kneel here, right now, and ask the Boss upstairs to help us," I advised frankly. "You don't want to wreck your marriage, do you? It's worse than cracking up this bus."

"I know. But what can we do?"

"Ask the Boss to help us line up the program—where we go, what we say, what we do."

"Okay, if you say so."

For the first time in my life I saw a broad-shouldered, powerful man in uniform kneel on a bus floor. I knelt beside him and prayed. As we stood, a mother and child approached and Harry rolled open the heavy door.

"I'll see Laura on the way home," I told him. "I'll let you know how I find things."

"Wish you would, Pastor. I don't want to lose her." The door squeezed itself back into place and the vehicle, with a roar like a volcano, struggled up the grade and into the congested highway.

I had a heart-to-heart talk with Laura twenty minutes later in the spacious, tree-shaded yard of an old New England farmhouse. I asked her to speak plainly. Were the four boys too great a burden? Was the father-in-law difficult?

"No, but Harry is selfish, obstinate. His eye is on the dollar, his . . ."

31

I stopped her. This wasn't the Laura I knew. For eight years she had attended the summer camp which I served as state dean. Her smile had brightened the days, her laughter charmed the nights. Her round, intelligent face was always aglow, her voice bracing as cool wind, her disposition not simply agreeable, but obliging. Now, tears trickled down her cheeks and her lips struggled to keep their fine contours.

"He's—he's non-cooperative, Pastor, non-cooperative in the things that mean everything to a woman!"

"For instance?"

"He won't drive me to church. He's always got the car. He wouldn't come to church to see our baby baptized. When something special is going on at the church he always goes somewhere else."

I had wondered what had happened to Laura. She had thrived in the sanctuary like a plant in a greenhouse. She and Harry had purchased a house, but it was not so distant that they couldn't drive to Westminster Church occasionally.

Harry called at the manse two evenings later. "Harry," I said, "your big trouble is bad eyesight."

"Got good eyes," he parried. "Got to, to drive the bus."

"But their near vision is gone," I added. "Maybe the far vision is better."

"What do you mean?"

"You big chump, you've been married four years to a wonderful girl and you've never seen her!"

"What do you mean?" he demanded. "She's a right pert-lookin' package. She dresses snappy and looks the part!"

"Laura's not a bag o' bone and a hank o' hair!" I said. "She's like a little saint. And a saint needs nurture. She's full of heart and a loving heart must have climate!"

"Nurture—climate?" stammered the busman "What's this got to do with my broken home?"

"It's broken for lack of nurture, climate."

"Listen," he interposed with vigor, "I drive that bus all day, up, down, in, out, till I'm dog-tired. Then I come home, work the garden. Then for four hours I grind out gas at a station in Willimantic. I come home nights— and I drop!"

"I know. I know."

"And Laura expects me to drive her to church, to ladies' aid meetings, to skip the boys over to Sunday school. Look, on Sunday mornings I'm done in!"

"Yes, and so's your marriage!"

The truth is hard to speak. But sometimes only severe treatment can heal.

"But I do it all for Laura!" he insisted. "And she complains!"

"Laura doesn't want that kind of life. You're so tired you get fretful, jumpy. You bolt your food without a blessing. You tramp by in a huff if she reads her Bible at the table. You growl if she wants the church to bless the fruit of your marriage. You forgot your last wedding anniversary."

33

"I was so bogged down with bills, debts—getting on in the world. . . ."

"Would it be getting on," I asked sharply, "to leave *her* behind?" It was my turn to challenge Harry to listen.

"Harry, I saw an ad in your bus the other day: *The family that prays together stays together.*"

"I was never keen on sermons," he interrupted. I raised a finger to quiet his protest.

"It's not a matter of cant, ritual, liturgy, Harry. Laura is devout. She thrives on her faith, the gospel hope, the divine love. Her heart demands this climate. You've starved her heart to death, literally. You have refused to let God water it, and now her love is withering away.

"As Laura loves God, the church, devout people, the Christian ideals, there will be more of her love for you, the boys, for me, for everybody. But you've nearly killed that sacred, beautiful plant, Harry. I hope the roots are still alive, deep down under the hard, rocky soil. There's a chance."

Harry had walked to the parsonage kitchen. He reached for his hat. My wife looked sadly at him. She, too, had interjected a few words about Laura. In that tense, troubled hour a busman bared his heart to me. He sobbed like a baby.

"The other night my oldest boy ran from the supper table. I heard him choking upstairs. I went to his bedroom. My twelve-year-old kid was on his knees, all crumpled up, and crying. He looked up. 'Dad,' he said,

'I can't bear it, without mother. I want to pray. I want God to bring her back. Daddy, how do you pray? Tell me!' "

Harry's tears fell to the kitchen floor. "My kid asked me how to pray . . . and I couldn't tell him."

Never have I peeked through a chink in a fence to watch a ball game and gained such a view as I had in that humid kitchen. How empty the father's cupboard when a child came to him for real food.

"I think this is it!" I declared confidently. "This is what Laura has waited for, these many years. Wait until she hears that her Harry wants to teach his boy to pray.

"Laura's birthday is coming up soon, isn't it?" I asked.

"Y-y-yes . . . it . . . it . . ." he choked.

"Don't work on her birthday!" I ordered.

"But, the bills—"

A pulpit gesture silenced him.

"No more of that, Harry. Start creating the proper climate for your home. You aren't going to work on her birthday. Leave the children with your father. Off to the shore you go—swimming. Laura loves the Atlantic. A shore dinner with all the fixings, chowder, lobster, clam cakes. Then a boat ride. And pray for moonlight and a flood-tide.

"Sit in the sands, climb the rocks, hold hands! Study moonbeams, count the stars, take Laura's kind, clean, wonderful face to your heart. Be a kid again. Win her, woo her. Why can't you?"

Harry's silence was beautiful. He didn't have to speak. I knew exactly what he was telling himself. He waited at the door for a parting word.

"To a very favored few the good Lord offers the second spring. You know, Harry, I believe you're on the good Lord's preferred list."

He shot a hand into mine with a force that penetrated my vertebrae. In two weeks summer was a-comin' in, and the home of Harry, Laura and Company would be a wonderful, wonderful place.

The Valley
and the Vision

Down in the valley, the valley so low,
Down in the valley I heard the wind blow....

IT WAS A SHARP, bitter wind of skepticism and criticism. And the man's father had taught the New Testament and pastoral theology in one of the nation's foremost seminaries.

"You should get to meet Danny," said the hill people to me not long after I moved into the little white parsonage. "Hope you can do something for him. He's been the despair of our last three pastors. You'll like him, but you'll meet your match!"

With more than usual curiosity, one bright spring day, I went to the small cottage, a solitary gleam of civilization in an elegantly contoured valley enshrined by trees and vocal with bird songs. Smoke curled into the still frosty air from a frame building behind the cottage. A man was boiling down the free-running sap. He smoked a long-stemmed pipe.

"So you're the new minister here," he greeted, studying me the way a dog watches an unknown human being. "Have you come to convert me? Time is precious, my friend. Better spend it on those who will respond."

Danny was lithe, six feet tall, perhaps forty-two years of age. His voice was musical, his eyes a piercing coral-sea blue. His unmanageable hair struggled to become brown, unable to fling off the spell of red.

His tiny gray-green cottage was a miniature library. Shelves lining the walls of four cluttered rooms were filled with books on science, philosophy, poetry, religion. "You have an excellent religious section," I observed.

"Yes. The volumes were my father's. No doubt you know of him. I didn't follow him—I'm the ugly duckling. I've read all his books. I fear some of his rather skeptical ones made me a skeptic. Father was strong and they didn't influence him. I decided not to accept the religious bunk!"

"I guess I caused Father no end of trouble because I didn't want to wear the cloth. I wasn't cut out for ladies' aid meetings, afternoon teas, social glamour, or for keeping a few neurotic millionaires comfortable!

"My socialist ideas weren't popular in the seminary two decades ago In spite of Father's influence, they threw me out. It killed Mother, I guess. *That* wasn't any help to me—any means of grace.

"Father managed to keep going another dozen years. He built this place and left it to me. So, here I stay—

with the trees, the birds, my library and some good pipes."

When I left the cottage I was deeply concerned. The bachelor son of a famous theologian had turned infidel— scorning his father's faith, silent about his mother's piety. One of his statements followed me home like a persistent ghost: "I wish no part in the great tragi-comedy called Society. I hate it and it hates me. I find peace only when left alone with my woods, my birds, my library and some good tobacco."

When I ventured again into the shadowed valley, it had become a sunburst in the explosive beauty of summer. But the harsh winds that never seemed to blow themselves out still buffeted me.

That afternoon Danny bitterly denounced his seminary instructors. In his mind they were cold, cruel men and he said that they had taught him to hate by failing to teach and translate love into action.

I responded by telling Danny that I knew a kind, practical theology teacher who placed a motto on his study wall, a motto I would like to see in Danny's library.

"What would that be?" he snapped.

Remember That God Ruled the World Before You Arrived and Will Likely Rule It After You're Gone. Why Not Let Him Rule It Today?

"Hmm," he mumbled as he blew smoke rings across the kitchen table. "Not so bad. Not bad at all, if only one believed in God."

"You haven't been scientific in your search for God," I suggested.

"Science?" He seized quickly, severely on the word. "What do you fellows know about science? You, with your meek little essays, parsimonious prayers, slap-every-body-on-the-shoulder methods?"

"God can be approached scientifically. The Gospel of John unfolds the laws of this science as the *Logos*—the logic or science of God."

Danny was listening. He emptied his pipe, filled it again, bent his face toward a sudden spurt of fire and puffed fresh smoke spirals into the room. "Go on," he encouraged. "You amuse me. It is—really—a dreadfully dreary life here. Amusements of a rational nature are most rare. Proceed."

"You have never taken seriously the science of the Master—prayer, obedience, self-discipline, faith. You let people and books distract you. You have confused the disciples with the great, resplendent Teacher: Christ. You have bolted the ranks of the disciples. You have never really known the Master Himself. Instead you tried to use your good father's faith. His was remarkably outstanding, but he had to work it all out in living experience.

"You have never allowed the faith within you to work itself out. You just stopped believing, praying, obeying the Nazarene's law. You never truly *experimented* with His tremendous system of science."

Danny did not answer. He picked up a magazine and read aloud an article on the faults and mistakes of the Bible. When he finished, he commented, "That is what a wise man has to say."

"Yes, a wise man who never followed the star," I said.

As I was leaving him that day Danny quoted me some lines from a poem by Henry Hubert Knibbs:

> I'm strong for the man who named it,
> *The Valley That God Forgot.*

"People liked my father. They don't like me," he said.

"How do you know?" I countered. "You never gave yourself the chance of finding out. You have decided not to like people."

"Look at your good Christians!" he continued with vigor. "They avoid me when I go to the village."

"They do not wish to annoy you. They respect your sensitivity."

"The women stare at me as though I were an escaped convict!"

"I have heard women say that you are a remarkable man."

Danny's eyes kindled into good humor. For the moment, his manner was entrancing and boyish. "Thanks, Reverend, for those kind intentions."

"That, sir, is strict truth," I informed him. "A good woman to do the washing, to sew, to cook—and perhaps Paradise could be regained in the valley God forgot."

I quoted an ancient passage: *It is not good for man to be alone*.

"If only the women today were like my mother," he said, as if in reverie.

"They are—once in a while," I prompted.

The third time I called I found him reading in his rustic chair beneath three huge sugar maples behind the saphouse. He glanced up, grinned, and placed an open book on the grass. He was reading Renan's *Life of Jesus*.

"I decided to dig a little deeper into the life of this Galilean," he said. "He was a sharp, outstanding thinker, and no mistake, but He was deluded into thinking He was divine. A Roman gibbet finished Him. That's what society always does to any outstanding thinker." Once more he burst into a torrent of invective. He lashed out at the social order, at religious institutions, at people in general and in particular.

I looked up at the pleasant slopes, toward the thick trees lining the hills. "This ought to be a good place for fox hunting," I said.

The sudden shift in the wind surprised him. "Fox hunting!" he declared. "Of course there are foxes in those hills. Many hunters come here during the season. But why the sudden interest?"

"Because you could take a course in sharpshooting. Got any guns around the place?"

"Nope! Don't believe in firearms. I couldn't kill anything."

42

"You ought to get some of those foxes. They are certainly spoiling the vines here."

"Hmm," he mused again, following my thought.

"Foxes of ill will, foxes of the bitter past, foxes of fear and cynicism. This valley—yes, your life—could be beautiful if you could only destroy those little foxes."

Danny was angry. He lurched to his feet, pulled the pipe from his mouth, and thrust his hand toward the road. "Better go now, Cleveland! I hate sermons. I swore I'd never listen to another one. I meant it. I really *don't* appreciate your interest at all. Sorry. Good day."

I could do nothing but follow the direction of the merciless finger that pointed toward the hills and far away. A week or so later I opened a letter: "Stop by again. Father always said I was too explosive. Really, I am—a mite interested—in what you said. Do you suppose we could go fox-hunting some time?"

I called on Danny again and again. The winds blew less bitterly. He read three or four volumes on faith and courage which were selected from my own library. One day I reminded him that even a doubting Ernest Renan had to exclaim to his class of Parisian students: "Jesus Christ was an incomparable Man!"

I asked Danny whether he could tell me the precise size and nature of the gulf that separated an incomparable Man from the divine Son of God. The challenge to work out such an intellectual problem delighted him.

One day I discovered him poring over Dean Farrar's

Life of Christ. Another time he was reading his father's well-marked Greek Testament and he was surrounded by Greek grammars, lexicons and commentaries.

"Maybe there is a scientific approach to Jesus," he mused. "Maybe this Man and His message are timeless. His logic might still work. That would make Him a permanent *reality*."

Three long, arduous years passed and my visits to the valley were not infrequent. Finally, one early autumn afternoon when the distant hills stood like shimmering stacks of gold at the rainbow's end, Danny hurried to me as I started up the well-traveled path. He seized my hand and his face blazed with a glory that outshone the hills. "I've been fox hunting! And I've got them all!" he exclaimed.

My Desperate Vow

FOR WEEKS AND weeks a pastor may wonder when all will be well with his world. Do things ever reach the even keel? A solid month of headaches and heartaches in the parish seemed to be straightening out when a schoolteacher telephoned me.

"Do you know about little Brenda McCormack?" she asked.

"What about her?"

"She was run over by a coal truck today. She's in the Robert Packer Hospital."

"How badly was she injured?"

"Both legs are broken—pelvis, too. Back injured—concussion of the brain. Poor, sweet little soul!"

Five-year-old Brenda was a slight elfin child with silken, silver-blonde hair. She lived in a house on the outskirts of Potterville in a section called Shantytown. Her rugged father answered the phone when I called.

"Is Brenda as badly hurt as I have been told?" I asked.

"Yes, Parson. She has been given only twelve hours to breathe the breath of life. My sweet baby! My sweet

baby! It's terrible wicked to have her wink out like this."
The man labored with his words.

For two years I had contended with this huge, stout
farmer, begging him to bring his three little girls to the
church school at Potterville. "Too busy, Pastor, too busy.
I work the farm here, and I work in a mill in New York.
It costs somethin' to raise young stock for the country
these days—the kids, I mean. It's gettin' harder ev'ry
year to feed an' clothe 'em." Such was his invariable
argument.

Talking to him now, I sensed only his anguish. "I'll
see you at the hospital," I promised.

"Glad to have you, Parson."

The hour was late. I was tired, yet my words had
slipped out so easily. Later I wondered if that was what
the Good Master meant when He said it would be given
to us in hours of stress and strain what to say.

An hour later I entered the children's ward and saw
the robust man, and his short, sweet-faced wife standing beside a child on a white cot. Heavy casts covered
both legs; her head was bandaged. An ugly gash crossed
the chalk-white face.

I prayed silently, continuing an S O S I had begun
along the forty-mile length of rural road. The child was
so terribly crushed. She had been dashed across a country
road where she was happily at play. The driver of the
truck had suffered a serious heart attack immediately
following the incident.

46

But what to say? Words of hope, strength, challenge suggested themselves to me as I looked upon a man crying, trying not to cry, while his wife stood beside him, a vision of agony.

"I am going to pray. It is not easy, sir, to pray at such a time. When I pray, I will reach out for something to bolster my own faith."

While making my confession, I recalled a sentence from a Nazarene Carpenter who delighted in children. Like a bracing wind from upper Galilee, His words blew into my stricken soul: ". . . it is not the will of your Father which is in heaven, that one of these little ones should perish" (Matthew 18:14).

I turned to Brenda's father. "Would you make a vow to God, the heavenly Father, in this critical hour?"

He stared at me. I saw great, silent tears roll down his florid face.

"If you can't, I will make a vow for you—if Brenda recovers you will bring her and her two sisters to our church school. The heavenly Father doesn't want Brenda just to grow up—He wants her to become pure, noble, beautiful. I can find faith and courage in prayer if I can make your vow to the heavenly Father."

Neither parent could find voice in that tense, hopeless hour. Their anguished minds focused on a white cot, so I prayed for them, made the vow for them. I bent over and kissed the unconscious, pale face.

"She is such a dear child!" I said.

47

"Oh, my sweet baby!" sobbed the big man. A nurse hurried into the room and I excused myself.

One week later, Brenda was back in her cottage, with both legs in heavy casts, and scarcely able to move. There appeared to be no brain concussion as had been feared. Later the doctor said to me, "Children fool you. They go down so fast, but they come back so fast."

For weeks, Brenda lay on her stomach, strapped to a large, flat board. Her hands propelled her prone body about the floors of the cottage. In three months the laughing child and her two older sisters were attending our expanding Sunday school.

Sunrise for
a Doctor

HANGING ON THE wall of my parsonage is an oil painting
of Singing Beach, Manchester, Massachusetts. Every time
I look at the jagged rocks, the breaking waves, the sea-
green mist, I remember the sound of bare feet coming
across the sands. I can even hear a deep voice and see a
bald head touched with sunlight.

Oil painting, my hobby, has led me to many exciting
experiences. One particular summer morning, while on
vacation, I made an early invasion of handsome Singing
Beach to paint the ragged outlines of Eagle Head. I set
up my easel, made my outline sketch in charcoal, squeezed
various pigments on my palette, selected some camel's
hair and sable brushes and began to paint.

I was impressed by the loneliness of the beach at that
early hour. The sun hid behind the sea mist; the horizon
was a gray-green blur. I could taste the salt air, and I
heard a sort of music in the breaking waves.

"Ah, this is living!" I said, as my sketch began to take

on form and color. I was congratulating myself for finding such invigorating privacy, when I saw someone coming toward me, far up the shoreline.

I was surrounded by rocks and ledges which I hoped would seclude me. I do not like to be disturbed during the earlier hours of my painting. "Whoever it is," I thought, "won't be bothering with me." I turned back to my canvas and forgot the distant figure.

As I stood back for focus a few moments later, I saw that my intruder was a stocky, middle-aged man in a colorful bathing suit. The August air was chill that morning and I marveled at his courage.

When the man spied me, he cupped his hands to his eyes. "Hello there!" he called. "Hel-lo!" He stopped, a stone's throw away, scanned palette, brushes, easel, and said, "Oh, an artist, eh? Well, I won't trouble you." He ran toward the incoming breakers. As he rushed into the sea he dove, headlong into a white-foaming billow.

The developing sketch absorbed my attention and I was "lost" amid my oils, shades and brushes until the crunching sound in the sand, for which the beach is celebrated, announced my visitor's return. I glanced up as he approached. In profound silence he studied my impression of Eagle Head, the rocks, waves, and the sea mist now illuminated by pools of golden sun.

"Water's beastly cold!" he growled. "Fine for walrus, seals, porpoise."

"You are an early riser," I noted.

"Yes, and I see that I have company." His dull, gray eyes searched mine. He spoke with precision, in a booming voice. "You know how to take a stiff morning bracer, don't you?"

"I try to."

"Sea air, salt water—great medicines. Tone up the system. You enjoy nature?"

"Yes, for many years."

"Are you an artist?"

"No, a preacher."

"You?" He frowned, cleared his throat, and drew back a step. Through squinted eyes he studied me. "Yet you paint?"

"Even preachers have to relax, don't they? I studied art in Boston during my youth. Now it's my hobby."

"And you find time for art in a busy life?"

"When I'm tired, confused with social problems, jail visits, hospital calls, working with displaced persons, broken homes, juvenile delinquency, I come here for a day."

My companion seemed to look inside me. Color invaded his tanned cheeks, and I thought he shivered.

"Nature re-creates me," I continued.

"You might say that you are a sort of physician," he said.

"I have quite a bit to do with the cure of souls," I told him.

"Well, I am a doctor," he confessed. Abruptly, he

heeled about in the crunching sand and ran back to the noisy, inrushing tide. Again he plunged into an icy breaker.

Some twenty minutes later, dripping wet, shaking himself, and pounding his chest, he approached my easel again. "You come here often?"

"Occasionally—summers." I addressed the doctor with his own query. "How about you?"

"This is my first summer. I am a New Yorker. I'm vacationing with friends—patients—back there." He pointed over a tree-tufted hill. "You may laugh, but I am here for my health."

Recalling a passage from my Bible I said: "Sort of 'Physician, heal thyself'?"

"I guess so. Fact is, I'm fighting a nervous breakdown. Can't eat, can't sleep, terribly jittery, can't meet people. I'm only good for the bathtub!" He pointed to the ocean. "I've been trying that stuff for a solid month."

"With much success?"

"Water wasn't meant to cure psychosis." He paused. "Excuse me, I mean a bad dose of nerves."

A preacher is always a preacher and the plump little man needed help. A man in trouble is always a minister's patient. "Can I help?" I asked.

"I don't know. I've been trying to wash off a thousand things, and without making much headway. Man can't fight fate."

"You're a fatalist?"

"Naturally."

"Why naturally?"

"Because I'm a doctor, a scientist."

"I have friends who are doctors and scientists and they are not fatalists."

"Huh, I think you're a good tonic for me," he said, enthusiastically. "Go on."

I put aside my palette and brushes and sat beside him on a smooth boulder. "Well, my friend, every time I come here I find a brand-new sunrise, a new sea, new colors, fresh winds. I never find yesterday's shadows here."

Curiously he searched my face. "Yes, that is so," he agreed solemnly.

"That bathtub of yours," I reminded him, "is not exactly the same as it was yesterday. The ocean pours in with fresh, stimulating water from that far horizon every morning."

"Yes, that—is—so."

He became so deeply engrossed in thought that I returned to my easel and spread new colors on the circular palette. A moment later I heard him crunching in the singing sand behind me. His hand grasped my shoulder.

"Look, preacher. I've got to talk to you."

"Let's stroll a bit."

"Fine."

As we started up the beach he said eagerly, "Perhaps you can give me a good prescription. I could use one! I need something real and I need it now! Perhaps we didn't meet today—by accident."

"You are near the end of yourself," I said quietly.

"That's right. You see, I lost my daughter not long ago. She died in a car accident—after a wild party. The sun rose and set on her. I'm involved with a foolish young nurse. My other youngster is in medical school. My wife has grown away from me and gives all her time to clubs, organizations, committees. And—here I am, trying to rise above a tide that's over my head." Like a spent dog he panted for breath and gazed faraway, toward a misty horizon. He was, in that instant, a picture of utter misery.

"The easy way out would be to drift out to sea with the tide," I ventured.

He turned to me, and already he looked like a drowning man. "What else can I do?"

"Do you love the nurse?" I asked.

"Good heavens, no!"

"Thank God. Then there is still hope."

"Of what?"

"That you won't drift out to sea."

"But the dirty mess is there!" He shouted the words over the sound of the deep-drumming sea. "The shipwreck is my fault and nothing can be done!"

"Nothing?" I tried to say with my mind and heart the words my voice couldn't say. "Nothing?" I suddenly remembered a portion of a poem I learned in seminary:

54

> Wail not for precious chances passed away,
> Weep not for golden ages on the wane!
> Each night I burn the records of the day;
> At sunrise every soul is born again.

As the sun's golden rays scattered the last pockets of mist, the doctor sat listening like a church audience on a bright Sabbath morning. "Say, preacher, what is that?"

"Part of Walter Malone's poem, 'Opportunity.' Been a favorite of mine for many years."

"It's not bad. Really, I like it. Say it to me again. A darned good prescription!" The quatrain was repeated. He grunted satisfaction.

"You neglected to burn the old records last night," I reminded him. "Here it is, sunrise. Why not be born again?"

"If only I could burn those old records, those rotten old records!" he cried. "I have some other records—of lives I failed to save. There was a wonderful boy, a baby girl, a fine woman." His fierce manner startled me. "Can you imagine what a doctor suffers when he uses everything he's learned—the latest in scientific discoveries—and still fails? Can you imagine the ghosts that haunt his sleep? All those old records, piling up, led to my breakdown—not just the loss of my daughter."

"We've got to burn those records," I persisted.

"How?"

"Burn them by putting them out of your mind. Yesterday died with yesterday. Can't you burn and bury?"

55

"At sunrise every soul is born again." He mumbled the words of the poem as he turned once more to the brilliant shore line, now a shimmering rainbow of color in the sunlight. Again he plunged into his ocean bathtub and I returned to place the finishing touches on my painting.

When he emerged he crunched through the sands to my side. "I've decided to go back to New York and clean up my shipwreck," he said. "I'll go to Boston, then on to New York. I think I might be able to burn and bury." He seemed to turn over those words in his mind several times before he said, "Your prescription is good —burn and bury. Let me have your name and address. I might have some good news for you. Let us see what the good Lord will bring forth."

I watched him as he slowly walked away. Far down the beach he swung about, his short, plump form casting a long, thin shadow along the sands. The bronzed hand he waved looked small in the distance.

A month later I received a telegram from New York: "Thanks. The prescription was good. There's medicine in poems. All is well. I have a new home. Yours, The Sunrise."

God and
a Teenage Girl

JACK EDWARDS WILL always insist that his life was saved when he spent sixty days in jail. There is no doubt in my mind that his sentence indirectly salvaged his little sister, Joyce.

"I had no work—had a car and needed parts for it. The only way to get them was to rob a junk yard." Jack told me a not unusual story about teenagers and their cars. It was a first offense for the seventeen-year-old stripling.

Jack did not particularly appeal to me until his last week in jail. He was bent over a game of solitaire in his cramped cell one Sunday afternoon as I moved in and out among the boys. He lifted his eyes from the cards and motioned to me to have a seat on the foot of his bunk.

"You know, Pastor, I wish you could help Sis," he said thoughtfully, flicking a strand of dark hair away from his right eye. "This little trip here has done me good. I don't want to be like some of these guys. I'm going straight from now on. But it's Sis that I'm worried about."

"Are you referring to a sister?"

"Yup, Joyce. Got five brothers, but she's my only sister. She's fourteen and she's in with the wrong crowd —smoking, drinking, swearing, out all hours of the night. She's giving poor Ma a hard time. I wish you could do something for her."

The boy had previously informed me that his father had died, most tragically, some years earlier. "Will Joyce listen to your mother?" I asked.

"Nope. I don't know what's come over her. Gee, she used to be a nice kid! Now she's going back on school. I'd like to beat up some of the guys who take her out, but they're too big. And I don't want to come back to this joint. Maybe she would listen to you."

"How long has Joyce been going with her wild crowd?"

"About three months. When Ma visited me last week she said that a couple of Joyce's friends used some awful language. Ma can't take it much longer. She says it's hard for a working woman to bring up a family and be both father and mother."

I spoke solemnly to the wistful boy. "Jack, if you really go straight and become a Christian, your example will help Joyce."

"I sure am going straight, believe me. But I think you

ought to sit down—like you're sitting down with me—and have a good, straight talk with Sis."

I promised him that I would.

"Sis is a real good kid at heart," the boy insisted. "All she needs is a good talking to from a minister."

Two evenings later I went to Joyce's home in the poorer section of Norwich. I introduced myself as Jack's friend and spoke to his sister in a humble, threadbare living room in an upstairs apartment. The girl was surprised and puzzled when I opened an Old Book. I read the sublime words, "And . . . the Lord God . . . made . . . a woman . . . ," above the sounds of children, auto horns, city noises and whistles in the yards and streets below. Against the low, coarse, unspiritual life of the streets I pitted the strength and idealism of an Ancient Record.

My theme God and womanhood. "A woman—a girl —is made in the image and likeness of God, with vast spiritual values and treasures. She is made to know and love the good, the true, the beautiful, to share the experience of day and night with her heavenly Father, who is good and holy. God has a strong, noble Adam for every Eve who keeps herself fit for his gallant wooing."

I saw that Joyce was listening reverently. "There are those in the world who scorn God's great plan, who make of Paradise a place of ruin and shame. Do you not wish to honor the living God, Joyce? Do you not vote for the good life, to preserve the beauty and truth of the garden? Keep your splendid youth for the young man of God's choosing. If you do, he will come some day to claim you in the garden."

"I do want a beautiful wedding, a nice house, strong kids," Joyce confessed with a wistful glance. Earnestness clothed her rather plain face like a dim halo.

My troubles began when Joyce repeated her decision to the two ungainly young men who had been taking her out.

"I am too young to think about love," she told them. "I got to wait. I don't want to lose God and my Adam."

"What?" cried the boys. "What's that about God? And who in heck is Adam? Adam who?"

The sudden revelation of a reformed Joyce drove two angry boys to Brooklyn, and to me. At that time I was battling with a weekly newspaper. My Brooklyn church had been ruined by a hurricane, and I was publishing and editing the *Quinebaug Valley News*. What a time I was having! I had to get the stories, write the ads, work up a circulation department, find paper boys, get the copies upon news stands, mail out bills, get subscribers and collect for services rendered!

I was so deeply imbedded in work that I failed to notice a bright red and yellow roadster parked beside my driveway as I approached my house one night. Two young men in the front seat watched me while I carried two huge loads of newspapers into the house. Each week my wife and children inserted an advertising flyer between the pages of 2500 newspapers.

When I finished, two long shadows met me in the evening gloom.

"Who be you?" one asked.

"Didn't you fellows see what I was doing?"

"You was deliverin' papers, but you ain't no paper boy." One boy smoked a pipe, the other a cigarette. Both were under the weather.

Said the slightly smaller one: "We thought the minister lived here. We been waitin' an hour, but we ain't seen him. This don't look like no minister's place."

It wasn't. My family and I were living in the Hatch Cottage, which had been opened to us by a kindly, retired clergyman.

"What do you want with the minister?" I asked.

"We're goin' to beat him up," pledged the first. "He told our girl we was snakes in the grass!"

"He sure did," snapped the second. "Said we was the devil in the backyard."

Suddenly I caught the drift of things and decided to announce myself. "So you're the two fellows who have been teaching Joyce to smoke, to drink, to swear at her mother, to laugh at school?"

The taller boy turned to the other. "The paper boy sounds just like Joyce made the preacher sound," he said. "But this ain't no preacher's house, and that don't look like no preacher's car."

My old Ford was rather ramshackle. It had the proverbial beaten look from hard battles against spring roads and slushy hills.

"A minister wouldn't be peddlin' papers without a coat, and a hat, and a black tie," the second boy decided. "Mebbe his old man's the minister."

"No, I'm the minister!"

A bolt of lightning would hardly have fallen with more impact to the twisted driveway. If I recall correctly, one fellow dropped his cigarette to the ground. The slightly smaller boy lurched closer to his friend.

"Heh, look at him. We thought he was a small, old minister. We didn't figger he'd be big, did we?"

"Looks like he could handle himself like a real one," observed the other. "I don't know if we could clean him up or not."

"Make up your minds, boys," I challenged. "And remember that I've been a jail chaplain for nine years. I've helped the police handle fellows like you."

"D'ye hear that?" whispered the smaller one. "He's given them coppers a hand!"

The two roughnecks slowly began to retreat in the darkness.

"Be sure you don't miss when you take the first swing," I warned them. "I've learned a few tricks, myself. You two ought to be arrested. I have a good mind to go into the house and call the police."

"For what?" stammered the tall boy.

"For threatening me on my own property. If one of you makes a move toward me I can have you run in for assault and battery. You're disturbing the peace already."

"You'd do that?" hiccoughed one.

"Gladly! A night or two in the cooler would be good for you boys. Turning a fatherless girl against her mother, her school and a decent life!"

"Yup, that's him okay," cried the taller intruder. "That's just how Joyce spieled. He turned our girl agin us—he's the one!"

It was my turn to try to salvage the two intractables. Raising my voice into the night I preached a sermon. "You boys need to realize, too, that Almighty God is in the garden that is His world. If you destroy His garden and the fine girls He has made, He will curse you and the trail of the serpent will follow you all the miserable days of your lives!"

"He gives me the heebie-jeebies," shivered the first boy. "There it is agin—we're snakes in the grass. But the jail's only around the bend in the road, and I don't want to get mixed up agin with them coppers."

"Nor I nuther," mumbled the second.

"If you had approached my daughter the way you talked to Joyce," I said, "I'd have taught you both a lesson you would never forget. Boys like you are destroying God's green earth and our beautiful girlhood!"

"We . . . we gotta . . . get out o' here," prompted the tall one.

"We won't get nowhere here," confessed the second.

Two lanky fugitive outlines sank into a roadster. Muttering and grumbling, they slammed two doors and drove away. I never saw them again.

Joyce and her brother did not retreat. Today, Jack is

superintendent of a large church school in a beautiful seaport along the Massachusetts shore. He keeps a watchful eye upon some three hundred boys and girls. And never did children and teenagers have a more solicitous, efficient overseer.

My Friend Jim

"WHAT'S THAT?"

My wife stirred in bed and sat up.

"Nothing, the wind, probably," I replied drowsily.

"That isn't wind. Someone's knocking on the side door."

"You're dreaming. Go to sleep."

"It's somebody! Wake up!" Suddenly resolute hands shook me.

Grumbling about the unearthly hour, 1:30 A.M., I snapped on the bed-lamp.

"Hurry up!" My wife nudged me. "Whoever it is will be gone."

"What an hour for visitors!"

When I opened the door a few moments later, I stared at a tall, thin youth, with wind and rain in his hair. He was a completely drenched portrait of the dark.

"I'm drunk—can't get home," the voice blurted. The words sounded as though they were stuck to his tongue.

"For mercy's sake, Jim, what happened?"

"Out on a bat. Got into a scrape with Red and Mike. They stopped the car—threw me out. What a dirty night! Can't you get me home?" Jim's teeth chattered.

A thousand thoughts raced through my brain. Walk a mile on such a night, under street lights for only half a mile? With Jim in his condition? Suppose I should pass some elder of the church?

A gust of cold, rain-filled wind blew in upon the new living room rug. The windows rattled.

"Shut the door—please," my wife directed from the bedroom. "The carpet will be ruined."

"Well, if you can't help—forgive me for in-intrudin! Didn't know where else to go. I—" Jim lurched about and slid down the steps, crumbling into a heap on the cement walk. I tried to catch him before he fell, but I was too late. I yanked him to his feet.

"Never mind me. What if I don't get home? May-maybe I should join the water wagon. Who cares? Everybody says I'm no good." When he was free of liquor and bad companions, Jim was a promising young man. He edited the village weekly newspaper. He was a student at Yale; brilliant, a poet, an author, member of a wealthy family in a distant state. People avoided him because of his sharp tongue, and many labeled him a Communist because his strong social ideals were misunderstood. Recently, he had begged the governor's car and wrecked it while one of the governor's daughters was with him.

"I can't leave you now," I told him. "Wait!"

In a few moments I was properly dressed for a bout

with the night. I grabbed Jim as though he were a foundering ship and pointed him toward the door.

"Come on, Jim. Cooperate, will you? I want to get you home."

He became almost a dead weight as I pushed, shoved and yanked him homeward through the fiend-driven night. Along the way I passed a dark, huddled form under a street lamp's yellow glow. A face was lifted and eyes peered out from beneath an oilskin hat.

"Gracious," I groaned inwardly as I recognized a leading elder in the church. The impact of this new personality seemed to revive Jim. He bellowed out the chorus of a loud, jangling popular song. I couldn't stop him.

In and out of mud puddles we splashed, slipping on the wet shoulder of the road and sprawling headlong into the rain-soaked brush at the roadside. Up and on again —to a large, red-brick tenement where Jim had his rooms.

As we stumbled up on the porch and stamped inside the entry, the landlord's wife called, "What's that?"

"Only the pastor. I brought Jim home."

Later, the landlord entered the bedroom where I had directed Jim and said he would take care of him. He and his wife liked the radical, rich youth, though they grieved for his philosophy of life.

I had once preached a sermon on the Good Samaritan and I got my call to follow his example on a terrible night in November. Jim's face revealed that he too had fallen among thieves. As it was, he contracted a heavy cold and narrowly escaped pneumonia.

Did the Good Samaritan undergo censure because he helped a despised and unpopular man? The question came to me when I was asked to call on the elder who had seen me with Jim.

"That young editor is a disgrace to this community," howled the irate elder. "He is always talking about socialism. I sometimes think he's a Communist. You had no business being seen with him under such conditions. Hellin' around, I calls it! Hellin' around!"

"But I was only helping him home."

"Would have done him good to lie in the rain. If he learns the hard way, he might mend his wicked ways."

"But he has been coming to church, hasn't he?"

"Yes, and two Sundays ago he struck a match right on the church building. He's no good, I tell you. He'll pervert the whole flock."

"Suppose he had been Arthur?" I said, a mite sharply.

In a firm voice he intoned, "My son would never be found in such straits. No, Pastor, you can't make your actions righteous in my sight."

Jim continued to come to divine worship occasionally, to please me, but he sensed the criticism that surrounded him. He said he always liked to get out into the free air. He came to the parsonage often and read me his poetry and listened to my piano improvisations.

Then one day we met on the street and he introduced

68

me to a charming, attractive lady, immaculately dressed and wearing a wide, flowery bonnet. "Pastor, I want you to meet my mother," he said. I shall not soon forget the respect and affection in his manner, the music he blended with the words, "my mother."

"I cannot thank you enough for helping Jim one night," she said. "I am a mother and I love Jim very, very much. I shall always pray for you and ask God to remember you. Jim will come out all right. I know."

Jim's mother proved to be prophetic. Although the newspaper folded up, Jim's friends at Yale advised him to reexamine his philosophy of life. After graduation he left New England and returned to the west where he is now a man of eminence and power. He is a district attorney and has a beautiful wife and five lusty, growing youngsters. He is also the Good Samaritan to all those who are lost along dark, wet roads.

Real Money

A HURRICANE THAT SCREAMED out of the hot Bahama
waters poured fury and destruction across New England,
our proud, lordly shrines its special targets. For once
New England pastorates became rare theological ban-
quets. So many were trampled out of existence that a
good church, like the proverbial good man, was hard to
find.

For four years I wrote sermons and made of a humble
rented cottage a shrine. A parlor table became a sacred
desk, and my wife and four children were my weekly
audience.

Years earlier my father had said to me, "Never beg or
borrow. Never receive charity for yourself that should
go only to those worse off than yourself."

Without a church, how would we break even in a
world of bills and taxes? For a while I was manager of
the record department of a large music store in eastern
Connecticut. Just barely did I eke out a living for my
wife and a foursome of growing children.

Into this hour of gloom walked a strange, swarthy
man. He bought records for nickelodeons.

"Play quite well don't you?" he commented one day, as I ran a tuneful song across the ivories for a customer. For several months he talked music to me. Then one noon hour he called to me from across the sunny street.

"Hey, there, Preacher-Man, I'd like to have a few words with you."

He was short, heavy and dark-skinned, and he wore an overpowering hat. He always wore an immaculate dark suit, gleaming white shirt and snappy black bow tie. His tweed coat was expensive.

We went into a nearby restaurant.

"I've got your story from your boss. Your church was crushed, you have four kids and you're really down on your luck."

"Not altogether."

"Let me talk," he continued. "This is, of course, confidential. Now, I need a good man in my business—a man who knows his music, likes it—a man I can trust. How'd you like to work for me? Go to Boston, New York, buy records, take care of my machines? You will be collecting nickels and dimes from cafes and restaurants. I think I can trust you. How about it?" He named my salary. He would supply a brand-new car and expense money. He literally smothered me under an avalanche of benevolences. When I hesitated, he paused, lit his cigar and smiled as the smoke rings curled mysteriously upward.

"My last two men couldn't be trusted," he mused. "I let them go. I have a way of checking on my men. I could have prosecuted, but didn't. Now that I think about it I believe an ex-preacher would give my business prestige."

"Not an ex-preacher, sir," I interrupted. "I am waiting for a pulpit. They're rather scarce in Connecticut at the moment. Hurricane, you know."

"Sure, I know. Sorry if I spoke out of turn. However, I made you a good offer, did I not?" His black eyes gleamed through the cigar smoke. "You need some hard cash, don't you? I know your take-home pay. Painfully inadequate," he all but whispered.

"The job would be a great help right now," I confessed, "but—"

"But what?"

"I don't relish the idea of going into beer gardens."

"And what's wrong with a glass of beer?"

"For eight years I served as dean for the Connecticut Youth Temperance Council."

How he laughed! "I'm in business to make money," he said. "Listen, Preacher-Man, when I wake up I think of money. When I eat breakfast I'm planning new plates for the cash. At dinner I'm dreaming up a new feast of money. After I read the evening paper I work up new markets for music. How do you think I get money? I think money, *money*, night and day."

"I awake thinking of God," I responded, "the God who gives me His treasures of life, health, family, friends, the Christian faith." He started to grin, and I stopped him.

"I think of God when I eat. I bless Him for ears to hear the music we both enjoy. I bless Him for eyes to

73

look upon His wonderful world, for soul to feel the love in it. I often go to sleep remembering that we share the amazing, beautiful universe—God and I."

My friend's eyelids blinked across his large eyes. His lips moved nervously. His cigar went out. When he recovered poise he re-lit his expensive cigar angrily. "Preacher-Man, you mean those words. Do you still believe them with your take-home pay, your cramped cottage and your four hungry kids?"

"I do."

"Okay, but I still need a business manager. And if you'll start thinking about money, for a change, you'll do better. Give me your answer in two weeks."

"I don't fancy emptying juke boxes in beer gardens," I repeated.

"It's all perfectly legal—the state says my business is okay. Don't be cranky about details. Go home, talk it over with the missus. She can use some cash."

I knew what my wife would say before I broached the subject at the supper table. How she stared at me.

"You—emptying machines in those places? Would you take me and your children with you? No, you should not accept his offer, though we could use the money—Priscilla's shoes, Wendell's shirts, Bruce's suit for school." She glanced at our invalid son. "And Rupert's pajamas!" She began to cry and ran from the table.

"Daddy, what made mother cry?" our youngest boy asked.

74

"Never mind."

Two weeks later I gave my answer to my would-be employer. In one word he gave me his opinion: "Fool."

A few years passed, and we lived in the Congregational parsonage on Westminster Hill, Canterbury. One afternoon I recognized a short, plump figure beneath an overpowering hat. It was the nickelodeon operator, still enjoying his cigar.

"Well, how do you do, Preacher-Man. How is everything going?"

"My daughter attends the seminary, training for religious work. I have a fine country church with good, country people. My wife has gained new health and my boys are joining the church. I am very happy. God is good. And you?" I inquired.

Pain turned his swarthy face into a sea of sorrow. "You ... you didn't know? Didn't see the papers?" He coughed violently and snapped a cigar stub into the gutter. "My only daughter was killed in an automobile crash with her boyfriend last year. My son—he is in my business—he's got too much money. He's drinking. I had to retire him. My wife grieves all the time."

As he spoke, he reached into his pocket. Slowly he brought a huge roll of bills up to his eyes. He held out a twenty-dollar bill. "Listen, Pastor, do me a favor. Take this. Go back to that country church, and say a prayer for me. . . ."

New-Mown Hay
and Healing

In every pastor's life there is a desert of experience—
a score of hard years when he wonders whether he has
really accomplished anything for God's Kingdom. Perhaps he even questions his once-eager call to the Christian
ministry. Like the heroic, exiled Moses he appears to be
marking time in the howling wilderness.

During a melancholy moment some lines of Lord
Byron came to my lips:

> My days are in the yellow leaf;
> The flowers and fruits of love are gone;
> The worm, the canker and the grief
> Are mine alone.

"You certainly don't sound like a preacher of Christ!"
my wife scolded me, as she clattered about the kitchen.
"You remind me of that old hymn, 'Hark! From the
Tombs a Doleful Sound'!"

"Tell the truth and shame the devil!" I countered with
one of grandmother's favorite axioms.

"Silence is sometimes *golden*!" she declared. "You, only thirty-six, talking like that!"

"The lines are from Byron's poem, 'On My Thirty-sixth Year.' "

"You're not Byron!"

Then one dark morning my wife stepped downstairs to find our youngest boy, Linwood Victor, dead in his cradle, victim of a thyroid gland infection. Grim shadows covered me, and I listened for the Master's voice.

For three days following our baby's death my wife said little to me, for she knew that I was unusually depressed. But on the fourth, when she heard the clattering blade of a farmer's mowing machine in the adjoining hay-field, she spoke. She must have read my thoughts, for she suddenly pointed to the sun-haloed field. "Look, darling!"

She beckoned me to her side. "Look." Her hand, like a magic wand, directed my eyes to a homespun silhouette looming against the golden walls of the morning. A hard-working Connecticut farmer rode a careening mowing machine, following a stolidly plodding gray horse. The man's blue shirt was open at the neck and his sleeves were rolled up.

My wife rolled up the window and breathed deeply. "What on earth?" I stammered, gazing at her.

"Inhale, darling!" she challenged. "Inhale! Isn't it wonderful?" She breathed in the delicious fragrances. "Didn't you once say that the first minister to the Massachusetts Bay Colony—his name was Francis Higginson, I think—didn't you say that he wrote to British friends

78

that a sip of New England air was better than a whole draught of old England's ale?" She grinned and added, "There ought to be more *back draught* to your sermons."

"Back draught?" I repeated.

"Yes, you ought to feel the power of the quotations you quote. Why don't they go back into the man in the pulpit?"

She pointed again to the open window. "Who would have thought such delightful odors, such beauty could be found in the summer grass—*when it is cut?*" She was so dramatic that I laughed in spite of myself.

"Yes, laugh," she sparkled. "But it's no laughing matter—*for the grass*. It's the cutting blade that releases the fragrance."

"What?" I stammered, for she was seldom so talkative.

"Grass is fragrant," she continued with rising emotion, "and becomes food for cattle *only when it is cut down*. Unless it suffers, grass cannot do good in the world."

My eyes wandered beyond the mowing field to the farmer's son, a mere dot on the landscape. He was raking and tumbling the hay mowed two days earlier. My wife watched the tiny outline. "When the grass is hurt, cut, dried, it is raked, stacked, and gathered into barns. Then it can help to yield milk and cream for our children in the bleak and crucial winter."

The wind rippled the tall grass. The field became an ocean of green waves that arched forward and bent backward in the golden sun. Sparrows circled overhead. The farmer lifted a bronzed hand and tilted his old straw hat across his brow. His hat, like a sunflower, followed the sun, protecting his head from hour to hour.

My wife placed a gentle hand on my shoulder. "There's a sermon for you."

"You think I need a new sermon?"

"Yes, I really do. Doesn't the good Lord cultivate us?" She searched my eyes, paused, and went on. "Sometimes I think He even applies the blade to make us scent the earth with the newly-released fragrance of faith, hope, love.

"After we suffer, we understand other people better. We feel with them and for them. Suffering seems to release deep, unknown sources of life and goodness and beauty within our hearts. Of course you know that." Her soft hand had slipped into mine. "Isn't that the meaning of the farmer? Isn't that also the meaning of the ministry of the Good Galilean you love?"

I had received more than a sermon, and a portion of a poem, a favorite with my wife, came to me in our kitchen making it a sort of sanctuary:

> The foolish fears of what might pass
> I cast them all away,
> Among the clover-scented grass,
> Among the new-mown hay,
> Among the rustling of the corn
> Where drowsy poppies nod,
> Where ill thoughts die and good are born—
> Out in the fields with God!

In that moment I had again grasped faith—and God!

80

The Magic Road
to Anywhere

And no man guessed what dreams were ours, as,
swinging, heel and toe,
We tramped the road to Anywhere, the magic road
to Anywhere
. . . such dear, dim years ago.

THE LILTING LINES of Robert W. Service echoed in mind
as I attempted to teach a difficult Sunday school class on
a breezy November day. We were trying, desperately, to
get a church school started and had drummed up a single
class, the ages six to seventy years. Inwardly discouraged,
I happened to gaze out a large church window.

What were those two intriguing shadowy shapes that
came and went among the little district schoolyard
swings? What, two thriving, lusty youngsters so close to
the church school and not in it? Here was a real lesson
for me.

"Who are those boys?" I asked my class. My daughter,
Priscilla, her two younger brothers, Wendell and Bruce,

another lad, a church clerk of sixty-five and Deacon Fred Hicks moved to the window.

"They're the Pahaikainen kids," said Wendell.

"That's Rusty and Tiny," added Bruce, six years old.

The boys across the road rested their bicycles against naked trees and climbed into two swings to beat fast tempo, heel and toe, with the strident measures of the brisk autumn wind.

"Look here!" I challenged my class. "So near the church and yet so far. Here's a rare opportunity for child evangelism."

I got no response from my congregation.

"I keep asking you fellows to recruit for the Sunday school, and what have you accomplished?" I said. My two sons received silent sermons from my eyes.

"Huh! I bet *you* couldn't get *them* to church," sniffed Wendell. "I asked 'em. No go."

"They're hard to get, Dad," warned Bruce.

"I could go right over there and bring those boys in here," I informed Bruce.

"Like to see ya," dared cynical Wendell.

"All right!" I turned to Priscilla and ordered, "Take the class!"

Scurrying into my hat and overcoat I tramped across the spacious churchyard, over the hard-top highway and to the small district schoolyard.

One boy was about nine years old, the other about five. They were swinging with amazing vigor. The older

82

lad continued his occupation, but the younger slid from his seat and hid behind a big maple tree.

"Are you Rusty?" I addressed the nine-year-old.

"Yup, I am."

"Come on over to Sunday school—you and your brother."

"Nope, don't want to."

In vain I tried to coax bashful Tiny from solitary confinement behind the tree trunk. I returned to Rusty.

"I'd like you to come over and meet my children."

"Nope, don't want to."

I had good records in salesmanship. Now, in twenty minutes, I scored incredible defeats. The older boy was adamant. The younger lad could have been a million miles away.

It was not pleasant to prove myself a flop in the eyes of my children. I felt all my sermons and lectures to them crumble in that rough wind. Finally, I stumbled upon a theme that never seems to fail.

"Like music?" I asked Rusty.

"Yup. My pa plays a sax in a band."

"Like hymns?"

"Nope, don't."

"Like patriotic songs?"

"Yup."

"Come across the road. We'll play some music. I play the piano."

"I don't know."

I sensed a shift in the wind and my own spirits rallied. Had a chance musical harpoon captured this slippery lad? Would his brother also come across the road?

Grasping Rusty's hand I helped him across the highway and hurried him up the thick church steps and fairly lifted him inside the building.

"We're going to sing!" I announced.

My class assumed places around the old upright piano.

"I like *Battle Hymn of the Republic*," Rusty suggested.

Once, twice, three times we sang it. We all but fought, bled and died singing it, until the rafters of the ancient Revolutionary shrine groaned beneath the burden of triumphant song.

Rusty returned to his swing after fifteen minutes. His little brother was still hidden behind his protective maple. A handful of people walked along the road to worship service.

Next day I ventured down a winding rural road to inform the boys' parents of my Sabbath strategy. As he stood by a noisy, red chicken coop and listened to my story the handsome young Finnish father laughed and laughed.

"Why, I'd have bet my bottom dollar you'd never get Rusty inside a church!" he guffawed. "And I think you're going to get Tiny next Sunday. Rusty says your daughter's real pretty and you play the piano like his uncle plays the drums. I think you'll win."

"We ought to tune up sometime," I hinted. "Sax and piano can play the melody neatly and in tune."

"Why not?" The good-humored young man with the light brown hair, thin moustache, and strong, white teeth was weighing, wiping, sorting and packing eggs while he talked. The infernal clatter of a healthy hen-house added bracing overtones to the conversation. He grinned. "There's music in that racket," he declared. "Like to have a couple dozen cracked eggs?"

"Sure would. There's music, too, in eggs fried in country butter!"

Little did I know that I had met a man who was destined to play a major role in healing a hurricane-paralyzed church. Little did I realize when I asked Rusty and Tiny to leave their swinging and walk with me along the magic road to Anywhere that they would invigorate a country church.

The Greek Cross
on Westminster's
Steeple

It is an ill wind, it is said, that blows no one any good. The hurricane that reduced the roof of my Brooklyn church to rubble also twisted the steeple from old Westminster as a child tears paper from candy.

When I first stared on torn Westminster Church, a couplet from Dean Swift trembled in my mind:

> A beggarly people,
> A Church and no steeple.

Inside the edifice, just beyond two stout green doors, I stumbled against a huge chunk of metal. A 700-pound bell lay on the floor, its carriage gone, its tongue lying mute. The shrine had lost its Christmas carol, its Sabbath call, its voice.

In the sanctuary I saw an exquisitely lettered motto on the wall: GLORY TO GOD IN THE HIGHEST, AND ON EARTH

PEACE, GOOD WILL TOWARD MEN. Perhaps those were the words that aroused the countryside to save an imperiled shrine, brawny Mr. Pahaikainen lending a strong hand until the bell was ringing again.

As the skeleton of the steeple edged skyward a lean, solemn stranger descended upon me in the emerald-green churchyard. He squinted up at the wooden structure. "What you put on top of steeple when it is done?"

"Weather vane probably, a weathercock."

He stared now at me. "What you say?"

"Most Pilgrim shrines have rooster weather vanes on top of their steeples."

"Hen on church steeple?" he questioned sharply. "Canterbury has hundred thousand hens in coops. You think that maybe not enough? You got to put one on top God's house?"

The stranger's name was Maxim. He was from the Ukraine, of Greek Orthodox faith, and he was over six feet tall.

"I hear you rebuild steeple," he continued. "I like to give church a cross. Jesus built new world with *cross* on His back. Did He go carry *rooster* on His back? Why you put *that* on top God's house? I buy cross for church."

"I don't believe the deacons—the church officers— would allow that," I informed Maxim.

"Why not?"

"It is not in keeping with New England traditions."

He seemed not to hear me. "I give cross as memorial.

I grow old. I like to make Christian gift to American church. I come years ago to this country. Want to know why?"

"Yes."

"I object when Czar's friends shoot too much wild game in the forests, wild game the poor people needed. I object to big taxes, too, so I lose friends of Czar. Then, Communist come to see me. Ask me to join them, they are starting party. I say I do not believe in brute force, so I lose Lenin's friend. And so come over here. There was no party for me over there.

"I have store in Fall River many year ago. But city no place for children. I look around, buy farm in Canterbury."

"You would show international good will," I said to Maxim, "by presenting a New England church with a cross."

"Yes, I like to do that."

While deacons debated the amazing offer, I often visited Maxim in his beautiful peach and apple orchard. Trees were his obsession. A month later, I told him he was authorized to procure a suitable symbol for Westminster's steeple.

"That is good!" He all but danced among the peach and apple trees.

One night Maxim showed me his household shrine. In a room decorated with Russian art was a Holy Bible on a handcarved lectern, some icons and candles. A table displayed devotional literature and the window drapes and wallpaper carried sacred motifs.

"And your people—some call me heathen!" he exploded, laughing merrily. "What Man of cross say? Judge not!"

Weeks passed, months, and the steeple overshadowed a completed belfry, but the promised cross failed to arrive. The steeple jack approached me for final conference. "Tomorrow, Pastor, the staging has to come down. I've waited a week for that cross, and after tomorrow it will be too late to set it up."

That very day the Plainfield Railroad Depot informed me that it had a long, oddly shaped box for the church. The Waterbury copper and brass company had searched unsuccessfully throughout New England for the proper mold for a cross. Finally one had been obtained from New York City.

Maxim drove me in his half-ton panel truck to Plainfield and I helped him load the heavy box. We placed it on the wide church steps as the steeple jack raised his wrecking bar against the steeple scaffolding. I shouted to a shadow aslant the sun, "We got the cross!"

He hurried down and into the vestibule where recently a broken bell had rested, denting the floor. He ripped open the box. "What on earth? This isn't a cross!"

Maxim explained with fervor, "It is the double cross of St. Andrew, a Greek Orthodox cross, just like the one on church where I go as boy." He pointed to an inscription on the copper base of the cross: "To the glory of God." How well it blended with the Old English lettering of the inscription inside the church.

In bewilderment I gazed at what seemed to be a skeleton of a cross, a wraith of the true symbol. *That . . .* on our church steeple?

Sudden, emergency sessions of the congregation were called. In the midst of heated debates, I overshot my own province. "That cross goes on the steeple or I resign!"

It wasn't long before a gold-leafed Greek Orthodox cross shone from the top of an aged Pilgrim shrine. Months passed before the New England villagers could adjust themselves to the unfamiliar shadows of St. Andrew, but time can shape beautiful world brotherhood out of copper—if the metal is in the form of a cross.

Little Girl Lost

LYRIS WAS A NAME I had never heard before I met the lovely thirteen-year-old girl. The name indicates a poetic, singing creature.

Lyris was fair, with clear blue eyes and long flaxen hair. Her voice was like the music of running brooks.

Lyris sang in the junior choir and had been coming to church from a considerable distance for a year. I had not suspected trouble at home until one Sunday afternoon when the junior choir went to sing at the Second Congregational Church in East Haddam. The other teenagers were in the sanctuary, ready to begin the service. Where was Lyris? I found her asleep on the back seat of my car.

"Hey, it's time for church!"

"It is?" she mumbled. "Am I tired. I can't get enough sleep lately. Daddy's away, my sister works, Mother is sick—and I have so many things to do."

Such exhaustion in a girl usually bursting with vitality disturbed me. Her question, a few weeks later, startled me. We went to East Haddam again and Lyris remained in the car until her pals piled out. Then, with a childlike frankness, she said, "I don't believe my father loves me."

Everyone knew that Lyris' father was her hero. He was tall, dark-haired, handsome and well-mannered. "Why?" I asked her.

"If my father really loves me, why does he leave me and Mother all the time?" I noticed that her name came first, and her sister was not mentioned. "Why does he leave me all the time?"

"Does he really leave you all the time?"

"I ought to know. He goes out with a young woman. He went to California with her—Florida, too. She even drives by our house in her car and honks the horn for him. What do you think of that?" She spoke with artless simplicity. "If my father doesn't love me, perhaps nobody really loves me."

A pastor can sense a lot of crying need in a snatch of conversation. I knew that our church had a real problem on its hands.

Lyris' father was a salesman who seemed to cover all parts of the nation, and I had a hard time finding him at home. Five weeks later, by a complicated table of computation, I caught him home at supper time. He was in the bathtub, calling for a towel through a closed door. When he finally emerged into the living room, where his thin, sickly wife sank into a soft sofa and his two girls watched television, I had a painful duty to perform.

I had to ask a spoiled man to reform. We had words— hard, brutal words. The wife, a sweet, long-suffering

94

woman, wept. The girls took sides for and against their mother, their father, and the parson.

Finally I repeated what Lyris had confessed to me. "Brother," I challenged, "your daughter's love for you is the one precious thing you possess and I hate to see you toss it away." I quoted Jesus about not giving that which is holy to dogs and not casting pearls before swine. "Don't lose your daughter's beautiful trust," I pleaded.

"Oh, Daddy!" Lyris cried, "I love you." With a startling outburst she flung herself at his feet and clutched his knees as though she were sinking and his body were a raft. I forced open the father's hands and wound them around his girl. Then he broke down. Father and daughter mingled tears of pain, sorrow, joy and hope. The older girl sobbed in her mother's arms.

Lyris begged her father to come to church with her and he promised he would come soon. He said he would live up to Christian ideals. For a few weeks the girl's face was like a precious jewel. Turn it any way, at any time, and it sparkled. Then, one Sunday after the congregation had dispersed, she hurried over to me.

"Can you help me pray, Pastor? Daddy has gone off again. We don't know where. But God knows, doesn't He?"

"Yes, the eternal Father knows."

"I want to ask God to send him back to me." Something old and very wonderful spoke from a little girl's mind and heart.

Lyris walked down the long aisle and knelt, her long hair flung across the scarlet seat of an altar chair. As she touched the floor she began to cry.

What could I do but kneel and place a fatherly hand across her shaking shoulders? I thought of my own little girl.

"Dear God," she wailed, "please send my daddy back to me. I got problems, dear God, and once Daddy helped me with them. You know how I really need him. Wherever he is—"

Sobs convulsed the devout little teenager and her tears fell to the scarlet carpet. When she arose, comforted, she smiled and said sweetly, "Daddy is coming back soon. God told me."

Two weeks later her father entered the upstairs apartment and broke bread at the family table. And then, not long after, there were words between husband and wife, and a frantic telephone call from the young woman. Once more Lyris' father went away.

"Come at once. We are in trouble," Lyris' mother telephoned me.

"My husband says he is involved with the other woman," she told me when I arrived. "She is going to have a baby, and will not release him. He wants a divorce."

"You see what good your talks did, your prayers!" shouted Lyris, a fierce light in her eyes. "Where is God now? Daddy's gone—for good! I don't believe in your God any more!"

Futilely I tried to stop her determined departure. Slamming the door she clattered down the steps and hurried away, crying as she ran.

Three months later her mother called me again. State authorities had arrested Lyris for riding around all night with noisy, intemperate boys and girls. The brutal facts were hard to accept. Not this—not this of Lyris!

A final phone call came from a policewoman who confronted Lyris with a list of miserable exploits. A physician confirmed Lyris' misdeeds.

I spoke to the girl in her home just before the policewoman took her to a state refuge for heedless girls. "Aren't you taking your Bible?" I asked Lyris.

She glared at me and said coldly, "No." As she left with the policewoman, she shouted back at the top of her lungs, "Who cares? I'm just a juvenile delinquent!"

In the state institution more sinister girls told Lyris about antics that horrified her, but soon she was listening, sharing the bravado, insolence and rebellion. Slowly the deterioration of a God-breathed life went on.

Where was Lyris' father? I heard he had gone to New York—New Jersey—Maine—but all efforts failed to locate him through charitable channels. His wife refused to send out an order for his arrest.

"He came back before," she sobbed. "He will come back again. If I have him arrested he will never come back to me. I know him. I will gamble on the chance that he will tire of this latest adventure and return. I will hold the door open.

The frail little woman had lost her appetite when she lost her husband. She lost interest in her home and it looked untidy. She appeared to lose interest in life itself.

"What happens to me doesn't matter. Who cares, anyway, for a sick wife? I'm not much good to anybody now."

"You've got to be patient," I said to her one day.

"Pastor," she replied with a half-smile and sad eyes, "my patience is clean worn out."

The man of the house vanished, and to this day no one knows where he went. The great world swallowed him and his illicit sweetheart and all the ominous shadows of the future.

The mother of Lyris became a mental and physical wreck and sank into muscular dystrophy. The older girl rushed off to marry a youth no one knew. Lyris passed to and fro beneath the challenging beauty of Maxim's cross on Westminster's steeple, but she did not come inside the church. For her there was no miracle.

Sometimes, when our pastures turn gray in times of drought, we pastors need someone to offer special prayers . . . for us.

Jacob's Ladder

WAS IT SIMPLY coincidence that I happened upon these lines by Edward E. Paramore, Jr.?

> Oh, tough as a steak was Yukon Jake—
> Hard-boiled as a picnic egg.

A few days after reading them I met him—if not the original Yukon Jake, at least the third or fourth edition. His name really was Jake, a lumbering log-roller of Alaskan winters and Swedish-Finnish background. He overshadowed a rural road like a tremendous piece of Alaskan timber, rising up to six-feet-three, solitary and sovereign in its own right.

The way his neck and shoulder muscles rolled together reminded me of a Guernsey bull. His hands, people said, fell like sledge hammers and I was to learn that he was "hard-boiled as a picnic egg." But let us begin at the beginning.

A simple Bible verse had been in my thoughts: "One ordinance shall be both for you of the congregation, and also for the stranger that sojourneth with you, an ordinance for ever in your generations: as ye are, so shall the stranger be before the Lord" (Numbers 15:15).

Were the strangers in our midst at home in our Pilgrim congregations? Did they worship as equals? Or were they considered outsiders and invaders? When I thought about my credentials in this world, I knew I should pay a call on the lumberman who lived on the country road.

"Hey, Jake."

"Mornin', Pastor."

"How about bringing Rinto to Sunday school?" Jake was very proud of his six-year-old son, the one child that attended his marriage made late in life.

"Don't know, Pastor. Got many cows, chickens, eggs. Don't know."

"I'll make a deal with you, Jake."

"What kind of deal?" There was a rich baritone timbre in the lumberman's voice, and his short, sharp sentences fell with the ring of an axe.

"Well, you bring Rinto to Sunday school and I'll consider it a personal favor. Then, when you need a personal favor, well—just collect."

After he thought a moment he shoved forth a huge hand. I felt the impact of steel in his grasp. "Okay, Pastor, we make deal. Mebbe . . . sometime . . . I . . . need . . . preacher."

Our deal went well for six months, until one furiously hot July Sunday morning. Jake brought his boy to the white church steps, as usual, and then he beckoned me aside.

"Pastor, we make deal, eh, what?"

"That's right."

"We need preacher . . . picnic grounds this afternoon. Fifteen hundred Finns be there . . . the reds, the whites, the blues."

"Sounds like the American flag!" I said.

"No. Red Finns are Stalin men. White Finns are Hitler men. Blues are nationalists—they blue because Stalin bomb one end of Finland and retreating Nazis burn other end."

"What about the picnic?" I insisted, mystified.

"Well, we hire speaker from New York. Police find he spoke for Communists. They tell organization that own picnic ground—if he speak we cannot have picnic. We tell speaker go home. I tell committee mebbe you speak, we have deal." His bright blue eyes searched mine relentlessly. "Mebbe you not . . . dare . . . to come. Your people not like. So . . . I excuse deal."

"Oh, no," I retorted, adjusting my black tie and fussing with my white collar. "A deal is a deal. I will speak."

"Mebbe you have trouble."

"A deal is a deal," I concluded.

He grinned, shook my hand, and said, "I tell committee," as he stepped into his car.

The Finns were celebrating their annual field day, an event which often ended in lively combats among the various factions. At the picnic grounds there was a track for sulky racing. At two-thirty the stands were filled with people, and the sun poured down upon the wooden pavilion where I stood. Sweat drenched stern committee faces. A sea of strange, critical faces billowed before me like ominous waves about to fall in paralyzing breakers all over me. I had tucked a speech inside my Bible, but one glance at the tense crowd and my speech was forgotten.

The local farmers had suffered in the fall from markets so poor that cabbages, sprouts, and cauliflower had been left to rot in unharvested fields. Despondency walked the countryside, burning up all possible encouragement.

I, a minister of Jesus Christ, faced lost, hurt sons of the soil, surrounded by their wives, children, parents. What could I say? How would I begin? How could I reach that restless throng?

My theme was simple. Jesus of Nazareth, a poor carpenter, was the friend of hurt, defeated people. All the real friends of Jesus feel for His people. The church should help men to live the more abundant life that is always attainable in God's world. I told my troubled audience that we must all pull together to build a better world.

Sweat drenched me and blinded my eyes. My stiff, black tie drooped into a formless rag as I used all the powers at my brief command to win the attention of people who came to see a famous Finnish orator and found an unfamiliar minister thrust upon them.

I tried to take all their worries, sorrows and tragedies to my heart. When I finished, literally panting with the heat, the stands rocked with thunderous applause. I could scarcely believe my ears.

Jake's iron hand hit my right arm. "That good, Pastor. I never forget."

Two weeks later, following a rural life seminar, an important dignitary of the church stepped over to me. "Cleveland, what is this I hear about your providing entertainment for a communist picnic?"

"A what?" I gasped.

"Did you know that you made the headlines in a Finnish newspaper of questionable loyalties? They call you Pastor Cleveland, Friend of the People." I had not known that a reporter from my own state had heard my speech and sent off a sizzling feature to a Finnish newspaper.

"Cleveland, what did you really try to say?"

"I told them that the church is a good shepherd who wants to help them find pasture. I tried to befriend those people—the reds, the whites and the blues. I told them to come to church!"

"Then forget the whole thing. We all would have tried to do as much."

Later, at secret organizational meetings, Americans were warned that a certain Connecticut pastor was becoming a dangerous radical.

However, from the day of the picnic, a sun-drenched man of black cloth had real work cut out for him, marrying, burying, trying to console reds, whites and blues in his liberty-loving and greathearted New England.

I kept in my mind the lines of Emma Lazarus that are engraved on the Statue of Liberty:

> . . . Give me your tired, your poor,
> Your huddled masses yearning to breathe free,
> The wretched refuse of your teeming shore.
> Send these, the homeless tempest-tost to me,
> I lift my lamp beside the golden door!

I had honestly tried to lift that lamp in a fearfully depressed countryside.

The next time Jake stood at the parsonage door, his tremendous hand on a little lad's tender shoulder, he said, "Pastor, you will please baptize my boy . . . a . . . Christian."

A Russian,
a Reason
and a Recruit

IN THE SUNLIGHT of the noisy schoolyard across the road
from the Congregational parsonage, I spied one day a
strange girl, nine or ten years of age, tall, stately, with
light brown pigtails and cheeks ripe as berries. She moved
with amazing delicacy and grace. I inquired about her of
the teacher.

"Her name is Lillya. Her father is Russian, her mother
is Latvian. They moved here from New York and took
over an old, run-down farm on a back road." Scenting a
new recruit for the church school I decided to venture
up an unfrequented road one afternoon.

The short, plump little mother was genial, but in no
mood to talk. "You must see Petya. He is in a back lot
chopping wood." She gave me directions, and I made my
way through straggly fields and tangled thickets. The
ringing of an axe guided me.

Suddenly I came upon a clearing and a mountain of a man, dripping with sweat and sunlight. He was perhaps six-feet-two, neither thin nor stout, muscular, with close-cut hair. He was looking my way, one hand cupped to his eyes to shade them from the hot sun. In the other hand was an axe. Trees sprawled all about him.

"You want . . . to see me?" His voice was deep and strong, everything about him screamed power and confidence.

"Yes, I am the minister from the church on the hill. I wanted to talk to you about Lillya."

"I do not care for church, pomp, ceremony. Why do you come here?"

"Well, you have a fine little girl and we all ought to worship and—"

"I worship!" His words were swift and sharp, like the axe he held. "I worship better than you!"

I stepped forward and shoved forth my hand. Slowly he accepted it.

"You . . . soft. What you do . . . with pale, weak, woman's hand?"

"I am an artist as well as a preacher. I like to keep my fingers supple and wrists flexible for a little piano music."

"You . . . paint? You . . . love nature? You love . . . the hills?"

I sat on a great tree stump and we talked. Our subjects were the vast, beautiful woodland, fireplaces and— art.

"I got to finish work," he said abruptly. "Much work on farm. Try to fix up old house, plant garden, prepare fields for cattle. You have to excuse me."

"What about Lillya for the Sunday school?" I urged again.

"No, she be all right here with her mother and father."

As I started away he called after me, "Maybe you come again some time, after chores, when we have more time and we talk . . . art?"

Two weeks later, my wife accompanied me as I again visited the young Russian's acres. His wife was delighted to greet a woman visitor. Soon, light refreshments were served, and then Petya nudged me into his room. It was filled with exquisite photographs of men and women, children, trees, landscapes, horses, sheep, cattle.

"I am New York photographer and illustrator," he explained, "but the city is no good for growing. So I come here. My girl sickly when young. Doctor said country air make new girl out of her. She love nature, flowers, birds, horses, dogs, cats."

"She takes after her father," I suggested. He smiled and began describing the various colored photographs. He told me about his friend, who was a wonderful artist, and showed me a group of paintings, symbolic and moving. I told him they were studies by Boris Artzybasheff.

"You are right," he enthused. "You are smart for minister. How you know Boris?"

"I don't. But I've seen his paintings on *Time* magazine covers and in other magazines. I know his style."

"He is great man. You like Russian art?"

"Very much. And Russian literature—Tolstoi, Gorky, Chekhov, Gogol, and, above all, Dostoievsky."

"You don't think we are all Bolsheviki?"

I laughed. "Of course not."

"Huh, I do not believe in church, sermon, tax money to church. Yet you do not think me Bolsheviki?"

"Of course not. You are just a little mixed up."

"Mixed up?" he echoed.

"Yes. You think I ignore your music. Why, I have met Sergei Rachmaninoff, my favorite composer. Where is there a more majestic musician than Peter Ilich Tchaikovsky? I have many recordings of music by Borodin, Rimski-Korsakov, Gluck."

"You . . . strange." His keen eyes seemed to look into my soul. "You like beauty . . . and music, and yet. . . ."

"Yes, Petya, and in Christianity I find the highest beauty and the superlative music."

"You find . . . art and music . . . in old dusty things like village churches?"

"No, in Jesus Christ!" I retorted, gathering strength.

"You . . . mean . . . that?"

"Jesus really called Himself the beautiful shepherd, according to the Greek. It is curious and wonderful to trace the concept of beauty through the New Testament.

And what of the angel's words over Bethlehem? Carlyle said that the speech of angels is music."

Petya bent his square head in deep thought. A full minute passed before he spoke. "Jesus Christ can teach beauty and make good music?" He had come to a turning point in his life when he spoke those words in a humble ramshackle farmhouse.

One thing bothered Petya—the fact that a minister did not know how to do "hard work." So when he invited me to learn the practical art of wood chopping, I accepted, although I was not very eager.

He gave me my first lesson with a two-man saw, a sharp axe, a splitting axe, a sledge hammer and wedges. The second lesson was somewhat dramatic.

I was talking to him about his favorite subject, nature, when I dropped my end of the sharp, heavy, two-handed saw. It struck his bare right ankle and blood oozed from a deep wound. Instead of tending his foot, he picked up my end of the saw and stared at the teeth to see whether I had injured the cutting blade. He shook his foot.

"It is nothing," he sighed. "A flesh wound. Nothing." He looked sadly at me and said something I will always remember. "A workman should have respect for his tools."

His words lingered in my memory. Did I, as a minister, respect the sacred Scriptures, prayer, my books, faith, hope and love, as much as Petya respected his saw and axe?

One time Petya invited us to supper, and the outdoor feast, Latvian-style, was unforgettable. Lillya hovered about us, listening to our conversation about nature, beauty, the great Spirit in creation and re-creation, and the melodies of the Christian religion.

All summer the visits continued. Petya had almost no other company. His criticism of modern life in New York had alienated most of his companions and his contempt for social customs made him a willing recluse. He was lonely, but he never would have admitted it to me or anyone else.

Then I reopened the Second Congregational Church, Millington Green, East Haddam, where once the famous pioneer missionary David Brainerd had preached. While calling in the rural area there I met Mr. Boris Artzybasheff. He made a donation to the shrine and his wife served us refreshments under the flower trellis. I could not wait to tell Petya.

"You—you talked church and faith and God to Boris?"

"Yes. He is a charming man."

"Tell me all about my countryman!"

"He has a studio, a little, square white building beyond the house. It has excellent light. In utter isolation he creates his masterpieces. Nobody can enter that studio while he works—not even his wife."

The following Sunday a tall girl with cherry cheeks and pigtails shyly approached the church and asked to be given a class. An hour later, and fifteen minutes late,

Petya and his wife slid into the very last pew in an old Puritan sanctuary and listened to gospel hymns, prayer, choir, sermon and benediction.

Today Petya will argue unmercifully with anybody who contests that the basic thought of Christianity is supreme art. He finds haunting music in the words of the Carpenter of Nazareth.

A Believer
in Karl Marx

DESTINY SOMETIMES MAKES us brothers. So I learned when I was asked to call on Karl Gottlieb, the sheep farmer. A neighbor said, "You see Karl. He is one strong man. He believer in Karl Marx."

"Is he Russian?"

"No, he German. You find out."

As I approached the huge barn and farmhouse a flock of white sheep loomed into view in an apple orchard. Thick, impenetrable woodlands surrounded the pastures and farm.

I parked my car and knocked at the back door. In the country a front door is only a convenience for out-of-town guests. A middle-sized, buxom woman answered my summons. Her blue eyes were animated beneath a thick aureole of hair twisted about her head in elegant spirals. I said I had called to invite her and her husband to church.

"Huh," she chuckled, "you wouldn't want my man in church."

"Why not?"

"The roof would fall in. We're German. The people call us Nazis." Her eyes sizzled. "Some people slam doors in our faces when we peddle strawberries, raspberries, apples, peaches. Some have thrown rocks at us. One man hurled a knife at me."

"But you are not Nazi?" I interrupted.

"No. Karl's father was a fervent Marxian. We feel that Russian communism is not a logical unfolding of the teaching of Marx. Karl despises Hitler!" She spat out the words.

"Your husband wouldn't come to church?"

"I doubt it."

She invited me into a spacious kitchen where we talked for a few minutes. Then she called to someone walking past the windows. "Hello! Karl! We got company."

A tall, well-knit man in homespun approached me with a hand thrust out. He wore a checkered cap and smoked a long, tapered pipe.

"The minister on the hill, Karl."

He squinted at me, puzzled. "How you find my place?"

"It wasn't hard."

Soon he spoke his mind. "You . . . capitalist. Your people . . . own everything."

"What?" I shot back. "Did you see that old automobile parked in your yard? That is all I own in this world. The church belongs to the congregation and my little parsonage is loaned to me." I lit into him. "You, sir, are the capitalist!"

The man staggered as though I had dealt him a physical blow. Then his body stiffened, his mind rallied. "What you mean?"

"You own this fine farm, and your sheds, garage, car and beach wagon. You own sheep and orchards and pastures. You are the capitalist, sir!"

He smoked a full two minutes before attempting rebuttal. Slowly he withdrew the smelly pipe, grinned and declared, "You are right! Hildegarde, hear him! The American speak true." He chuckled merrily.

We were not making progress toward church, however. When Karl left the room to hunt for a stack of magazines, his wife came over to me and asked, softly, "Did I hear that you play the piano?"

"Correct."

"Karl isn't a bad violinist. You'll never get anywhere with him by arguing politics or religion."

She led me to an old-fashioned upright in a friendly-looking parlor. I fussed with the keys and was going over some Stephen Foster melodies when Karl returned. Suddenly a wonderful idea struck me. I began to play a tender, little German folk song.

Mrs. Gottlieb uttered a delighted outcry and said to her husband, "Karl, you hear that? Get out your fiddle." She began to sing the German words to "*Du, Du, Lebst in Meinem Herzen*" ("You Live in My Heart").

Karl laid a violin case on top of the piano and tugged at instrument and bow.

Sensing a bit of victory, I commenced a second

German folk song, "*Ach, Wie Kann Ich Dich Verlassen*" ("How Can I Leave Thee?"), the sweet love song of Thuringia. Karl tuned his violin and joined us.

As we finished I spun around on the piano stool. Mrs. Gottlieb had relaxed into a parlor chair and was drinking in the music. The tall shepherd smiled. I recalled a sentence of Jean Paul Richter, one of Karl's countrymen: "It sank into his heart, like the melody of a song sounding from out of childhood days."

"You know 'The Beautiful Blue Danube'?" Karl inquired.

"A favorite!"

Again he slid his fiddle under his chin and swept the bow across the strings. Karl really worked to make the Danube roll. He soon had it leaping and tumbling and pouring in cadenzas and arpeggios. The moment I caught up with one zestful measure he moved into faster tempo.

Then I saw that Hildegarde was whirling and bobbing about the room. As the waltz increased in tempo she laughed and swung into faster steps, pirouetting, flouncing, tap-dancing. As she spun among chairs, floor lamps, book cases, on rugs and on the bare floor, the elegant spirals of hair vibrated on her head, in rhythm with the waltz. "Ah, this is good!" When she had spun herself out, she dropped into a rocking chair, convulsed with merriment.

"Whew! Whew!" she exclaimed, fanning herself with a magazine. "Just like 86th Street! This was rare!"

116

Finally Karl and I got the Blue Danube under control and we stopped, both in a dripping sweat. We looked as though we had just been pulled out of the river.

"My! My!" burst the shepherd. "I worked harder in the past ten minutes than in my four hours in the hayfield!" Tenderly he placed the violin in the case and tucked the bow beside it.

"Pastor, how about a glass of cold beer?" Karl asked.

"No thanks. The Blue Danube stuff is good enough for me."

"Good ginger ale then?" Hildegarde suggested, rising.

"That would be fine."

With a chuckle Karl reached for his pipe and sat in the overstuffed chair. "What your people say if they hear that?"

"You mean the music?"

"Yes."

"They would like it."

"And they not call us Nazi, throw rocks and make children scream at us?"

"My people have brains. They like good music. Why, you might play some Sunday with me—'*Eine Feste Burg Ist Unser Gott.*'"

"Yes, I might play Martin Luther's hymn, 'A Mighty Fortress Is Our God.' That, too, is good music. Why not, Hildegarde?" He paused as though surprised. "You think I, Karl Johann Gottlieb, follower of Karl Marx, could play music . . . in church?"

" 'Workers of the world unite; you have nothing to lose but your chains.' " As I quoted that famous sentence from Karl Marx, the shepherd stared and gasped. He yanked the match to his lips and blew out the flame—it had burned his fingers.

"I learned those words when I was in theological seminary, in a sociology class."

"You learned . . . that . . . in school for ministers . . . in this country?" he stammered. "This is strange country."

"It's a wonderful country, Mr. Gottlieb."

"You call me Karl, eh, what?"

After his beaming wife served an excellent lunch she asked, "Would you both please play once more, *'Du, Du, Lebst in Meinem Herzen'*?"

As I returned home late that day, words from Ralph Waldo Emerson echoed in my thoughts:

> For the world was built in order,
> And the atoms march in tune,
> Rhyme the pipe, and time the warder,
> The sun obeys them and the moon.

Soon Karl was playing a German hymn in church, and when his Communist friends objected, he answered, "It is better to go to church and hear sermon and play hymns than to go to Communist picnics, drink beer and fight!"

He resigned from the Communist party, joined our congregation and eventually became our Sunday school superintendent. He is in his favorite pew every Sunday, among friends and neighbors who join in the worship services of the world. He listens attentively to the beautifully appealing words of the good Man of Nazareth, whose gospel, not the dogma of Karl Marx, can save the world.

Finnish Steam Bath

PAPA VASA LIVED in the northernmost extremity of North Society Road in a Finnish colony on the rural fringes of an old Yankee township. He and twenty-five other Finnish farmers polka-dotted a twisting road along which they sent a hundred thousand broilers each day toward the carnivorous New York markets.

Papa Vasa hailed originally from the Gulf of Bothnia in northern Finland. Ice and snow were the familiar accompaniments to nature in his homeland.

I first saw him in a littered back yard. A crutch was tucked under one of his arms, and he navigated on one leg, followed by two dogs—a huge brown-and-white St. Bernard and a small black mongrel—two frisky pigs, a turkey gobbler, a half-dozen sheep and lambs, gander and geese, and cats galore.

Papa Vasa did not talk—he issued orders. "Come with Papa. Come get dinner. You boys, hurry along here. Don't hard-press me. Don't be so noisy!" He shouted above the barking, gobbling, squawking, ba-ba-ing, grunting and meowing. A cut-off trouser leg swung back and forth as he bobbed along on his crutch.

I was fascinated as I entered the yard. "Hel-lo!" I shouted, and instantly the two dogs started for me.

"Back! Back!" A stern voice commanded.

The dogs stopped, tossed up their heads, ears, tails, and dashed back to stand by the one good leg of their master.

"You fool—to come in yard!" he said. "You supposed to stop at house. Wife, girls, they send for me. We do not let strangers in our back yard. You go in house. I be in when I feed my boys."

When he came in the house, Papa Vasa exchanged the crutch for a cane and sat in a big lounge chair. Immediately the black dog leaped upon his lap, but his eyes watched me. His manner was in no sense congenial.

"Nobody can come near me when he stands watch," smiled the Finn, "not even my children. He good boy, good soldier." As his heavy, sun-bronzed hand patted the black head, the dog's fierce eyes surrendered to affection until he seemed to smile. In the next instant the militant creature stretched toward me and growled.

"No, no, Baron!"

"Baron?" I questioned.

"Yes, named for my commander in old country, Baron Von Mannerheim. Years ago, when young man, I served under him."

He observed that I had noticed his affliction.

"Trouble start, I think, when I was young—wounded in battle. Leg never right. Last year I went to Finland

again and it begin to ache bad. Doctor there say he cut
it off. But could I leave my leg in Finland? No. I tell
everybody I take back to United States everything I
take out of United States." His laughter came in strong
gusts and he thumped the floor with his cane.

"You say you minister? Where you live? Why you
come here? For donation? We poor people, we not
church people."

"No, I did not come for a donation. I come from the
big, white church on the hill."

"Hurricane play tricks with your church—twist head
off!" he announced. "That big wind . . . like Gulf of
Bothnia—not even care about church." With his cane he
struck at a cat that had come too close to the black dog.
The large calico cat scurried for shelter.

"Why you come?" He turned again to me.

"To get acquainted. I like to know who lives along
the road. I might be of use to you sometime."

"You—be of use—to me?" He laughed again and
tapped his shiny, bald head. "We not call for minister
here."

"You might need me sometime—for sick calls. Suppose
you should need a doctor? Somebody might ask me where
you live."

He knit his flourishing brows as he patted the black
head nestled in his arm.

"Mebbe. Mebbe not. But minister not much good for
people. Church not care for people. What your church

people care about chicken farmer? We lose money to raise broiler.

"You build big, new school. Build new road. Who care to build better market for eggs, roasters, capons?"

Wielding his hickory cane as he spoke, Papa Vasa thumped a table, a book, and the floor. "And what do you care about the poor?" He stretched his cane toward a black trouser leg. "Do you go to town meeting? You try to help dairy, chicken farmer? No! You preach sermons, you call on old ladies, drink tea, and tell everybody everything good, very good. Well, I tell you everything is very bad! You do not tell truth!"

Never had a man poured such invective and blame upon me. He looked out the great north window and patted the head of the dog stretched out in beautiful sleep.

"You know why I stay away from church?" he suddenly asked.

"Why?"

"In Finland we had state tax to support churches. If poor man have bad year, could not pay tax, I have known the church to take poor man's horse, cow, chicken to pay tax. Is that justice? Is that the truth your religion preach? Did the Teacher of Asia say thing like that, the Man you say started church?"

"I suppose we do not always follow the noble teachings of our Lord," I acknowledged.

The cane fell with less vigor and the blazing eyes gleamed less fiercely. Papa Vasa pulled a huge bandanna from a back pocket, and cleared his throat noisily.

"I like to see you be Christian," he said, "be man of truth, justice, logic. Why you not help poor man? Was not Teacher of Asia poor Man—Carpenter? Why you not go to town meeting, go to state house, look into politics? Why you not really try—try hard—to make world better?"

I was now taking stock of his mental merchandise—justice, truth, right, logic. These were the words of a thoughtful man, a courageous man, an heroic man.

"You too soft," he continued. "Need to be soldier for a while. Need steam bath to toughen you up. I tell you what. Come up some Saturday night to *souna*."

Next to his wife and children a Finn loves his *souna*, or steam bath. It is as much a part of the home as a kitchen or bedroom.

Papa Vasa gave the black head a nudge. "How is that, Baron? We see how soft he is, eh?" The dog stirred, raised his head and barked. "That good, Baron. You agree. We see if he can take test." He had made a lunge at friendship, and I had to accept the invitation or face an impenetrable wall.

Oh, that *souna*! We undressed and entered a tiny house of two rooms: the little dressing room and the steam bath. Seasoned cord wood heated a small iron stove, around which stones were piled. Two pails of cold water were near the stones.

When the stones became sizzling-hot, Papa Vasa ordered me to toss some of the cold water on them. Steam—fiery, penetrating, burning—filled the *souna*.

"That good," he muttered. With a genial grunt, he sat on a low wooden bench opposite the stones. I sat on a higher bench.

"Hah! You not be up there long," he warned. "You wait." He poured more cold water on the stones, and a dense cloud of steam rolled up into my face. I could feel it in my ears, eyes, throat, and even in the last, low disc of the vertebrae on my sheltered side.

"Hah, I show you how soft is minister!"

A still fiercer steam cloud rolled up from the volcanic rock and immersed us in choking, suffocating heat. I could scarcely breathe. Papa Vasa turned to me with a puzzled look in his eyes. "I try again!"

As the cold water hit the furious stones with a roaring noise, I thought of the vapors that covered Mt. Sinai—full of flame and terror. I was a burning sensation, from head to toe. I cupped my hands to my swollen eyes and dilated nostrils, trying to see and breathe. I was determined not to be blasted out of my summit intrenchments.

Red as a boiled lobster, the Finn pulled himself upright with his cane. He opened the thin, wooden door and vanished inside the dressing room. Ten minutes later he again pushed open the door and bellowed, "It is enough! We dress. Have coffee."

I endured the ordeal of fire and soon I was experimenting with Finnish bread, coffee cake, delicacies and coffee served to me in the big kitchen by Papa Vasa's wife and three girls. I also began to take more of an interest in town meetings and the plight of the poor, our humblest citizens.

At one meeting I spoke so vehemently for them and for just dealing with discouraged chicken farmers that a wealthy gentleman, an official on the town board of tax review, paid the manse an excited call. "Cleveland, you have this whole town in an awful huff. You've taken sides with the riff-raff! You've attacked all decent society. Your work is done in this community."

"The farmers should have their rights. I think the whole meeting was unfair."

I used the ammunition of Papa Vasa and I think my visitor sensed it. He literally jumped about in a rage on the porch as I said, "You, sir, can call the good citizens together any night that seems convenient to start proceedings against me. It might surprise you to find out who is going to be tarred and feathered!"

I can still hear his climactic "Oh!" as he turned tail and left.

Papa Vasa and a preacher became great friends. The coffee we drank together! The sweet Finnish pastries we consumed! He could not come to church because he could not sit comfortably on the hard pew, even though we overlaid it with cushions. Finally he asked me not to embarrrass him.

Years later I remembered my early words to him, "I might be of use to you sometime," when it became my painful duty to bury him, as well as his handsome, but alcoholic son. It was my joy to perform the weddings of his charming, beautiful daughters.

Papa Vasa was a man who could have added words of truth, justice and logic to the President's Cabinet. He resembled the great English prime minister, William Ewart Gladstone, and, under other circumstances, might have become a truly powerful statesman. He became, instead, a story in the annals of the poor.

At his brief memorial service, I hinted that, deep down, there dwelt in him a genuine, simple, heroic Christianity. He had more love for justice, the town and his neighbors than any of us ever suspected.

Before the flower-strewn lid was lowered, the old crutch was tenderly placed in the casket. One month later the little black dog rushed off into the thick, green forest behind the house and never came back.

Irish Cobblers
and the Inevitable

THERE WAS A MAN who had a happy heart only when he could give me a heavy one. I never knew anybody who so enjoyed putting a preacher to confusion. Once or twice a Psalm came to mind as I bent and bowed and all but broke beneath his onslaughts: " . . . O Lord. Let them be ashamed and confounded that seek after my soul: let them be turned backward, and put to confusion, that desire my hurt" (Psalm 70:1, 2).

Paddy and his wife lived on a remote tract of land. To insure comfortable privacy he had placed generous amounts of brushland and sproutland between himself and his neighbors.

Eastern Connecticut had no more industrious and successful vegetable farmer. He raised Irish cobblers, the sniff of which could whet any man's appetite. I can still taste the high-piled, downy-soft "smashed potatoes" his wife sent to the parish suppers.

In Paddy the church had its most formidable critic.

"So you're from the city?" he said when I tried to make his acquaintance. "City slickers don't know much. Now that you've moved to the country—because the city didn't want you any longer—I suppose you'll have a garden."

"No, not I."

"Why not?"

"Well, for one thing, I am a pianist as well as a preacher. I wouldn't want to injure my fingers."

He snatched the thin, yellow stem of his pipe from grim, set jaws and let fly the words. He didn't raise his voice, but the breath of his nostrils made desolations in the earth. "Afraid to hurt your city hands in honest soil? Do you know who pays your salary, Mister?"

"The church pays me."

"And who is the church here? Farmers who plant, fertilize and harvest the soil. Are you better than they? You take their money quick enough—which they scrape up out of the soil. Wouldn't hurt you a bit to get your hands dirty, Mister. If you want to reach farmers—have a garden!" He tramped away, throwing up a thick smoke screen. After due consideration I plowed and planted a garden behind the manse.

One day he drove his wobbling old truck along the road and I stopped him. I pointed to a shade tree in one corner of my garden. "What can I plant in the shade?" I inquired.

"Do you know what I'd do if I were you?"

"What?"

"Plant a chair," he grunted, chuckling, and stepped on the gas.

That was Paddy, always deflating my enthusiasm. Once, when he avoided Sunday morning services, I pressed him for a reason. He remarked that no man with horse-sense took time out on a busy day to listen to a man who didn't know the basic facts of farming.

"God made the land, Mister. How can tillers of the soil learn much from a man who doesn't understand God's original plan—creation of heaven and *earth*!" How he emphasized that last word.

I visited his lush rural acres and met his sprightly wife, his handsome collie dog, his horde of cats. But the visit made no improvement in his church attendance.

I tried to help him plant cauliflower. He relieved me after a few minutes because I didn't know how to set the plants properly and I cost him money. He stopped me when I tried to milk a cow—he said I got more milk on my shoe than in the pail. I tried to transplant strawberries —my pianist fingers were too clumsy. Another day I cut cabbages—I was too slow with the knife. Paddy called me an expensive preacher.

The crisis came on a glorious October day. I had gone calling along a picturesque back road and came to Paddy's farm in the afternoon. He was busy cutting and crating cauliflower. "If you want to talk, help me get these ready for market!" he ordered. For two strenuous hours I bagged and crated produce.

After the usual procedure of trial and error I learned

to stuff the right number of heads into a crate without ruining them. Fifty crates were ready for market, stacked on the farm truck.

"Bet you couldn't get up at three o'clock and follow these crates to market. A lot you care about the farmer's problems, you city slickers!" He grunted, smoked, eyed me. "I go to market every morning—have been—for a month. A neighbor boy used to go. He overslept twice, so I fired him. My wife can't go—she's not well. Bet you couldn't get up that early if your life depended on it!"

"Perhaps I could."

"What would the community think—you up at three in the morning, in work clothes, doing some honest work?" One had to study Paddy's lips to detect a smile.

Paddy was lame from hard work. Once he had ventured, "You know, Mister, each year I have to get up a little earlier, plow a little deeper, work a little later to make the profit that I made the year before. When I can't get up earlier, plow deeper, work later—I'm done!"

Now he had challenged me to meet him by the town's rotary at 3 A.M.

"I will," was my decision.

"We'll see," he grunted.

The country intersection at that unearthly hour was cold, dark and eerie, so I was not unhappy when two great orange orbs loomed from the thick darkness. An old noisy truck, its radiator steaming, came to a staggering stop at the rotary and a voice called, "Jump in!"

What a night ride that was, as a wheezing, choking old vehicle went fuming and frothing through the October darkness. We struggled and fought to make every grade, and plunged down hard-top slopes as though we were bent for destruction.

"You're a smart one," Paddy mused as faint tremors of dawn touched the horizon. "You're from Boston. Of course you know what a whiffle-tree is. You must have seen them in your trips around the country." He pronounced the word "whipple-tree," with emphasis on the word, "tree." I gazed at the passing landscape, searching all uprearing silhouettes. I asked whether he referred to some strange, country genus of lacy growth.

"It's a moving, wooden bar on a wagon," he snapped, chuckling. "See how much a city slicker knows? Any country boy knows what a whiffle-tree is!"

Nursing the wound, I lapsed into silence.

He spoke again. "I make good money in the spring, selling grass. Brings a good price early in the season."

"You sell—grass—in the market?"

"Sure. I cut it, box it, bunch it."

"Grass?" I cried.

"Asparagus!" he triumphed. "Any country boy knows what grass is!"

A minute later and he tried me again. "I wonder how a preacher would describe the difference between tame and wild hay?" Painfully I remained silent, but it would have been a massacre to become vocal.

133

When we arrived at the busy, noisy Providence (R. I.) market, I tried to help. I dropped a precious crate of cauliflower while we unloaded. Paddy spoke quickly to the market-boss. "Don't mind him. He's my new hired hand—from Boston. He hasn't learned his way around."

Paddy invited me to accompany him to breakfast in a restaurant thronged with farmers, truckmen, railroad men, and baggage smashers. "Flapjacks, applesauce, sausage, coffee," he ordered.

In my haste to oblige I ordered, "Applejack, pancakes —" It was the only time I heard Paddy really laugh. He caught at his falling pipe. "Applejack!" he grimaced, winking at the stunned man behind the counter. Then, pointing to me, he said, "He thinks he's in Tennessee, real thirsty, ain't he? He's new around here. Bring him flapjacks, applesauce, sausage and coffee."

He nudged me. "How do you want the coffee? Black, brown or pale-faced?"

"The way you like it."

"Two black ones!" he snapped.

Seating myself on a stool I started to remove my hat. His eyes caught mine.

"Don't take that lid off," he threatened under his breath. "Nobody does that here. Why, they'll all know you come from the country!"

At 8 A.M. Paddy again dropped me at the rotary.

"Well, Dominie, you survived," was all he said. Off he went in his shaking, wheezing old jalopy to his "bungalow," as he called his farmhouse.

"Dominie." The new word struck me like a thrilling chord. Was it sign of recognition? Did he believe that I had made the grade?

On the following Sunday morning a slim, shadow of a man limped into a back pew in time for the sermon. When I saw Paddy, big as life, in church, I knew I had passed all the road tests. From now on he would be riding with me.

"Old Turnip Top"

NEIGHBORS ON Tatnic Hill Road described him as "Old Turnip Top." It came to me, finally, why. His head did look—for all the world!—like a ripe rutabaga turnip.

His head was round, the yellowed skin overrun in the upper areas with a thick color, almost purple. His close-cut, stubby hair jutted up like turnip tops after the harvesting knife has clipped off the leaves. His puffy, sun-hardened cheeks curving down to a yellow, dimpled chin further enhanced the illusion. Sometimes I wondered if nature had not intended him for a vegetable rather than a man.

Nothing seemed to suit him and he certainly did not aim to suit anyone. He was considered ornery and obstinate. I knew I was only inviting trouble when I parked my car by his forbidding white fence. I saw his large figure in the yard.

"How do you do?" I saluted as I stepped from the car.

"What you want?" A face turned my way, and he was indeed "Old Turnip Top." "You want to buy cow?"

"No."

"Want to buy milk?"

"No."

"Chicken?"

"No."

"Egg?"

"No."

"Then you buy vegetable?"

"No."

"Then what you want?"

"I just dropped by to say hello."

He squinted at me from under bushy brows, and a strange, ludicrous light spread across the purple-yellow features.

"You want to say hel-lo to cow, chicken?"

"No. I am going along the road greeting the people."

"Why you greet people?"

"I am the new minister from the church on the hill."

When he frowned, the sagging eyebrows seemed to add menacing lines to his eyes. "You minister, eh? Then you no come here. I . . . hate . . . minister! They lazy, no good, spoil people." He spat upon the ground. "That . . . for you!" He bent to the earth, laboring over a brooder-stove and totally oblivious to my presence.

How relieved I was, driving away! I informed my friends at the supper table about my afternoon experiences, concluding that we just had to scratch "Old Turnip Top" off our list. Papa Vasa was a harmless schoolboy compared to him.

"But he has a girl, Olga," my daughter Priscilla explained. "She's in my class at school. She ought to be in the choir."

Priscilla's information encouraged me to make a second call on the surly farmer. I found him cleaning the barn.

"You come again," he growled. "Want say hel-lo?"

"I hear you have a daughter."

"Sure. Olga."

"She is my little girl's friend. Priscilla thought Olga might like to sing in the choir."

"Olga in church? Never! What is church? Place for old man to snore, place for old woman to chatter, place for new babies too small to know anything." He spat upon the smelly floor. "That . . . for church!"

I protested.

"Go on! Get out!" he howled. "Three year ago I order governor of state off my land. He hunt deer and I no want anyone hunt deer. This is my land. I no want you here. Get out!" He flourished the pitchfork at me.

Two months later, as I was driving along the roads in the rain, I met Olga on her way home from school. She had missed the bus and was reluctant to get into the car.

"Father will not like this."

"You're soaking wet."

"Father will not like this, me riding with a minister."

When we got to the farmhouse she bolted from the

car like a hunted fox and raced for the back door. Priscilla informed me that the kindness extended his daughter left her father entirely unimpressed.

Then I made my final effort. I had been reading Carlyle on heroes and hero worship, and a wave of remarkable confidence, or sublime audacity, broke over me. I hurried down to the forbidding white fence and found the farmer plodding toward the big red barn.

"Hi, there!"

He stopped, glared at me, and cupped a shaggy hand to shaggier brows. "You . . . here . . . again?" I will not attempt to describe the look on his face.

"Listen, friend," I fairly roared at him, "I feel pretty tough today and I wanted to tackle the toughest man in town. So I came here."

I didn't know whether he was furious, distracted or simply confused. Silently he searched my eyes.

"You know, we ought to get acquainted."

"We what?"

"Think about it. You're tough, but you're just a man. You could die. And you're so tough no preacher would bury you. You might rot on top of the ground. I think I'm the only man tough enough to give you a decent burial. Know that?"

I shiver every time I remember the presumptuous sins in my words. I expected him to charge me like the Guernsey bull I had seen in the barn, but he stood facing me, with his hands hanging, poised for action, at his powerful hips. And then he began to laugh. He was still laughing when his wife came hurrying out of the barn.

"Papa, what you do?" she cried. "What you do?"

"Preacher, here, he is tough, he is tough like Papa, only *he* put me in ground when the time come!" He shook with laughter as he spoke to his wife and pointed toward me.

"Papa, not say such thing," his handsome wife complained.

"Mama, if we be not nice to him . . . have minister for friend . . . what happen if I die? Mama want Papa to rot on green field? He say no other man bury me. And just you, Olga will be at funeral."

He came toward me with short, stern steps and to his wife's amazement he shoved out a heavy, hairy hand. His hand gripped mine like a thunderbolt striking.

"You . . . strange minister. But we be friend. Come to house, have cider and doughnut." And I did.

The farmer began to drive Olga to Sunday school in his big, shiny automobile, and his Sabbath jaunt became the talk of the town. Olga remained for the service and during my sermons she would often express her opinions aloud: "I don't believe it. It's not true. It's crazy!"

For weeks she parried my paragraphs from her vantage point in the choir, disturbing the whole congregation. But I had asked for Olga and I got her, plus plenty of her obstinate father in her! "Serves the preacher right for getting such people into the church," people said.

Like Papa Vasa, Olga's father never attended worship services. But he loved the old hymns. Many a cold winter night, after chores, he relaxed in a big, old-fashioned chair in the parlor. With eyes closed, he smoked dreamily while his wife, his three children, and a preacher sang such tender hymns as "Rock of Ages," "Fairest Lord Jesus," "The Haven of Rest."

Whenever we stopped he called for still more hymns. "They . . . make . . . me . . . feel . . . good."

Although we never got him into an old Pilgrim church, I have an idea that we fed him a lot of sacred food on those winter nights. And years later, when Olga married, Papa made it his stern business to see that she married a fine young man who went to church regularly and knew how to sing all the old hymns.

The Word
That Came Alive

A DEACON OF Westminster Church wrote me that Mrs. Timothy E. Hanley was very ill. "She would like to have the Holy Communion. You had better see her at once."

For years I had known the stout, genial, gray-haired lady who lived in an adjoining town. A servant answered my knock at the door and I was led into the sickroom.

"Pastor, I've been in terrible pain all week. My time has come, I know. Will you please administer the sacrament?"

The hopelessness in her words distressed me and I paused before unsnapping the black lid to the Holy Communion set. Sometimes, in such solemn hours, the poetic line of John Burroughs comes back to me: "I stay my haste, I make delays."

Pastors themselves face hard hours as they try to comfort the hopelessly ill, the dying. A pastor who truly bears the burdens of his flock must grow old before his normal span of years.

The despairing lady went on. "I want to go. My husband is well established in business. My son is well married. He has a wonderful government position in Washington. I am old and worn out, and I am ready to go. Please give me the sacrament."

"You should not try to upset the great Father's timetable," I admonished.

"Why, Pastor, what do you mean?" From the crumpled bed she studied me.

I quoted one of the Master's final sentences: "It is not for you to know the times or the seasons, which the Father hath put in his own power" (Acts 1:7).

"What has that to do with my timetable?" she exploded.

"Your husband has not been strong for the past two years and he certainly needs you. Your son sold a valuable invention to the United States army. He is walking on the high places of the earth and he needs the prayers and guidance of his mother."

"Pastor, I've lived a long, hard life. It is time God called me."

"Mrs. Hanley, I cannot give you the Holy Communion at this time."

"Why not?"

"The words Holy Communion indicate communion with the divine Father and submission to His perfect will. I am not sure that He wants you to die. You are discouraged because you have been very ill. But Holy

Communion is something to live by—the bread and the wine give us strength for the new day, the forward march."

When she accepted this simple, friendly philosophy, I handed her the bread and wine. Her lively Boston bull terrier sat quietly on the carpet as we prayed.

The prayer for new strength was heard because when I called again, two weeks later, Mrs. Hanley opened the front door, her face a bouquet of smiles. "Come in, Pastor. I am feeling much, much better."

Soon the special maid was no longer needed and in two months Mrs. Hanley was able to call on her neighbors for the first time in five years. She returned to her abandoned church duties and amazed the other good ladies. The despondent housewife underwent a change that only the word "metamorphosis" can describe.

Mrs. Hanley's husband had rarely attended church.

"I guess I joined the church because my wife did, many years ago," he once told me. "I've never been a man for sermons and all those things. I'm a salesman, a matter-of-fact man. Faith and prayer may be all right for children, cripples, widows, the aged, but not for a lively chap like me!"

He did begin to frequent the sanctuary when his wife's health improved. Anonymously, he sent the rural meeting house two cords of seasoned oak for the winter fires. And then his heart condition took a decided turn for the worse. I did not have to remind a devoted wife that the good Lord knew what He was doing when He spared her.

Big Tim Hanley fell away to half his size. Early one morning, against the doctor's orders, he crept downstairs while his nurse dozed. The next day his horrified wife and son saw that he had carried the large library dictionary up to his bed.

"For pity's sake, Tim, what are you doing with that?" his wife demanded. "Of all books! Prowling around at all hours for a dictionary! Your nightstand is piled with good, devotional reading."

"I just wanted the dictionary," he said.

Tim would close the ponderous volume whenever his wife, nurse, or son entered the room. They worried about the astonishing turn of events, but didn't dare to oppose him.

When he entered the hospital for his last gallant battle the big fellow had his nurse fetch the big dictionary. It rested on top of a stack of newspapers, magazines and prayer books.

"What on earth, Father?" his son exploded as he breezed into the sickroom one stifling day. His father had his good eye glued to a blurred page.

"I'm just checking up on Mr. Webster." He ventured not another word.

After Tim was buried, his disconsolate widow gave me the crumb of information which I craved. "Pastor, just before Tim died he told me something. He asked me to pray. When I did, I asked him why he had been reading the dictionary. He grinned—he knew he had us all eaten up with curiosity."

The widow tried to recall exactly what he said. "Wife, I saw something happen . . . to you . . . after you took communion in our home one day. And I just . . . wondered . . . after all . . . what it meant in this world . . . to be . . . a Christian. The big table dictionary . . . said . . . that a Christian is the highest kind of man . . . one who believes. . . ."

Big Tim would have said many more things in that beautiful, sad hour if his weakened heart had not suddenly imposed on an eager tongue a most profound, mysterious silence.

Double Wedding

MRS. ROBERT MANTON had attended church a score of times before I sensed the anguish and woe within her. We see as little of the human soul with the naked eye as we see of the great stellar spaces. One Sunday night came the disclosure.

It was the first evening service Mrs. Manton had attended and she came with her husband, a married son and daughter-in-law. She was, I should say, sixty-eight years of age, a mother of nine, a grandmother of eleven. She was small, plump and gray-haired. Her misty blue eyes were tucked away behind thick bifocals, and ragged teeth punctuated her poorly articulated phrases when she talked.

After the meeting Mrs. Manton and her three companions moved slowly toward the rear door and the vestry. Suddenly the woman burst into violent sobbing, and bowed her sallow cheeks in long, bony fingers as her plump body literally shook in a deluge of tears.

"My Beaky! Oh, my poor Beaky!" she wailed.

Again and again she choked out the words as though they burned her mouth. Her rounded shoulders bent in a tempest of emotion that frightened the retiring audience.

"What is it, Mrs. Manton?" I approached her and touched her shoulder. "What on earth is the matter?"

Awkward, convulsive moments passed before she could speak. Others drew near and stood helplessly by. Her husband stared at her, offering no word, as though he too were overwhelmed. Neither the son, amazingly large beside the stout, diminutive mother, nor the daughter-in-law ventured a shred of testimony.

Five minutes must have elapsed before the stricken soul could summon the will to talk. Her words became a tragic confessional spoken to the pastor and the small Christian circle, "after hours," beneath the hanging balcony, beside a dying, hickory fire in a huge, pot-bellied stove.

"Beaky! It's my pet name for Rebecca. Beaky's my youngest. I don't know where she is, who she's with, if she's sick, well, hungry, in a hospital, expectin' another young 'un. I don't know how the three she's already got are doin'. Oh, my poor Beaky!"

There are tense, dramatic hours when the greatest service a minister can perform is to let a member pour out the soul. He can only stand by and receive the bitter, staggering avalanche. How few church people realize, perhaps, the volcanic tides that roar down upon a parish pastor, stunning him, turning his own hair white as he tries to stop the white-hot lava that is thrust forth from boiling, hidden depths.

"And them three young 'uns love their grammy! Beaky was always so close to me! She might be in a hospital—she might be dead!"

Once more her voice was buried by a fierce outburst of tears. As the pain eased a little I said, "God knows all about Rebecca. He knows where she is, and whether she is all right. Why don't we take Him into our confidence?"

Mrs. Manton stared at me through the drenched bifocals. "You think—you think—it would—do any good —to pray?"

"Let's go back to the altar," I prompted. "Let's have a summit conference."

"A . . . what?" she stammered.

"A summit conference." I quoted a portion of Scripture, then reached for one of the Bibles in a nearby pew. "Let me read the 93rd Psalm," I suggested.

Fourteen or fifteen people stood in the aisle and listened to the reading of the Word:

The Lord reigneth, he is clothed with majesty; the Lord is clothed with strength, wherewith he hath girded himself: the world also is stablished, that it cannot be moved.

Thy throne is established of old: thou art from everlasting.

The floods have lifted up, O Lord, the floods have lifted up their voice; the floods lift up their waves. . . .

Thy testimonies are very sure: holiness becometh thine house, O Lord, for ever.

When I finished, the meaning of a summit conference was interpreted and the fury of the mighty waters had subsided. We all moved to the front of the Church for a New Testament reading. I pointed to the motto on the sanctuary wall behind the sacred desk: "Glory to God in the highest, and on earth peace, good will toward men."

Each member of the little flock knelt with me before the holy altar and prayed that peace might come to the stricken mother. As I prayed a certain thought was expressed aloud. "O gracious Lord, who reigneth in majesty on the throne established high above the bitter floods and the mighty waters, answer the cry of this poor woman. This year let her hear from Rebecca, wherever she may be, and may the news be not bad, but good. For the Master's sake. Amen."

Mrs. Manton pulled herself to her feet, her face aglow. "Oh, Pastor, do you think I might hear from my poor Beaky before the year is out? We're already half through November."

I had not wholly realized that there were only six weeks left in the calendar year. Was I trying to crowd the Lord into my own anxious schedule? For a minute it was my turn to tremble. I replied, "God can answer before New Year's Day if He wants to." A line from Emily Dickinson occurred to me, bringing its crumb of comfort: "When it's late for man it's early yet for God."

At 8 o'clock on New Year's Eve the phone rang in a mill village home in eastern Connecticut. It was a New

Year's greeting from Rebecca—from another state.
Years earlier in a Model T I had chased two runaway
girls along the starlit macadam roads of that same village.
Now another runaway girl made her first overtures of
hope, faith and love to a mother's home, and breathed a
daughter's blessing above those same roads.

The following Sabbath Mrs. Manton stepped tri-
umphantly up the church aisle with an astonishing narrative. She had waited until most of the communicants
left the shrine. Waves of sunshine poured from a glowing soul as she said, "Beaky is doin' all right. She's comin'
home. And my man and me, we want to get married—
to celebrate. We want to get married right here—in this
church."

"Then you aren't—aren't really Mrs. Robert Manton?" I gasped.

"No. Common-law wife. I buried three husbands and
I wasn't quick to bury a fourth. I thought I wouldn't
bother with all the fuss this time. My man's not been
much on church and sermons and prayers. But Beaky,
she's made a Christian out'n him.

"He went home and laughed about your prayer, and
God, and Beaky, six weeks ago. He said you was crazy.
But he's changed his tune. You oughta seed his face
when I told him Beaky was on the line and wishin' me
a happy New Year! He said he reckoned there was a
big Boss in the world after all, and if He knew our names
and street address so good, we'd better get hitched

proper. Will you marry me and Bob—right here?" Robert Manton had slipped noiselessly from the vestry into the green shade of the maples.

"Sure!" I answered. "So Robert thinks I'm crazy! Well, you tell him I'm crazy about big church weddings. Let's have a time!"

And we did have a good time—with bride, groom, children, relatives and friends by the dozen. But I doubt that anyone at the wedding was so thoroughly happy, so utterly delighted as the returned wanderer who was also being properly married—Rebecca!

Ten Little Hurricanes

It was a cloudy Tuesday morning and I was going full-tilt on the typewriter, forging a sermon on the power of God. A clanging phone shattered my spiritual train of thought. The call came from a distant acquaintance whose wife sometimes visited our sanctuary.

"Hello, Pastor. Say, my niece is in terrible trouble. She's got ten kids and the state is taking them away. She's in bad shape. I told her I'd call you. Was that okay?"

The note of urgency in his usually placid voice prompted me to leave an unfinished sermon and go forth to tackle the unfinished business in the world.

At exactly eleven-forty-five I nosed my car into a littered yard and knocked on a battered back door.

"Come in!" The voice was not steady.

I stepped into a kitchen that looked like the uneven floor of an old cargo ship. Water streamed over it from a pail beside one wall, and a huge woman mopped up one corner. The table and chairs were battered; so were the walls, the stove, the woodbox, and the woman. What casualty of storm was this poor, smashed vessel?

The mop, wringing-wet, released a stream of brackish water toward me. Staring at me, the woman uttered a weird cry. "Yes, you're the man! You're the one!" She turned to a small, fat woman who was peeling potatoes over a pail of water on the battered table. "Marie, that's the man I was telling you about!"

I stood as though I had been transfixed by a witch's spell. The big woman's tears dropped off the end of her nose into the pail as she said, "I dreamed about you . . . last night. I dreamed that God sent me someone to get me out of the mess I'm in. I dreamed that God would send him here this morning. In my dream you came while I was mopping the floor. And—look at the time."

Fearfully I slanted my eyes toward a clock on the mantel. The time was eleven-fifty.

"Morning's all but gone and this is my last corner. Oh, it's wonderful!" She wept with joy. Through her thick, oval glasses her snapping eyes scrutinized me and the yawning expanse of wet floor.

"You are God's man!" she proclaimed. "I did have a dream, and I saw you saving my kids for me. The state wants to take every one!"

I told her about the phone call and said I had heard that a court case was pending. Neighbors and school authorities had complained about the incorrigible offspring.

"It is terrible," she groaned.

"The church can help, can't it?" I cheered.

"The boys are tough and use awful words."

"The church can help, can't it?"

"My man and me, we do hit the bottle now and then. A body's got to have some rest from a yelling tribe o' Indians!"

"The church can help, can't it?"

"We got to face the judge."

"The church can help, can't it?"

"Who'd want my wild young'uns in church, no fit clothes or manners? Sent them once. Nobody wanted my poor young'uns."

"I want them."

"You . . . really . . . do? My Henry and Windy, my Bugler and Bob, my Susy and Nell?"

"We . . . want . . . them."

From the dilapidated three-legged table, the other woman spoke nervously. "My man ain't worked for months. We'll starve." Her tears mingled with potato peelings in the dirty water. Placing a hand on her dark hair, I prayed: "O Lord, Thy child is far from Thee. Give her man work . . . right away."

She covered me with incredulous glances. "But he ain't worked for months!"

Suddenly I heard a roar, a rumbling, thundering noise of a cyclone, and the outside yard bobbed with wild shouting faces. The back door banged open and a half-dozen separate hurricane centers invaded the kitchen.

"Kids! Young'uns, simmer down!" ordered a frantic mother.

"Ma—who is he?" each gyrating figure demanded.

"He's the man God sent to help us."

"Yah?"

"That so, Ma?"

"How come?"

"Why didn't ya say?"

Here was an entire church school in one huge, formless mass of delinquent, desperate children. Might not love be the Fairy Godmother who would wave a magic wand across the wet floor and transform a poor, smashed hull into a glittering ship filled with precious cargo?

Years earlier, when I was a young chaplain at the Roger W. Babson Institute, Wellesley Hills, Massachusetts, I received a valuable lesson in extra-curricular activities. One autumn afternoon Dr. George W. Coleman, eminent president, led me to an immense boulder on the green-fringed campus and pointed to a bronze tablet. "Read it, Cleveland," he urged. "You bit off a lot to come here and work with our boys. Read Mr. Babson's motto. It perked him up when he was a young man. He was ill, with one lung gone, and hurrying West to recuperate. These lines will stiffen you for the battle:

> Bite off more than you can chew; then chew it.
> Plan more work than you can do; then do it.
> Hitch your wagon to a star,
> Keep your seat and there you are:
> Go to it!"

In the dizzily whirling kitchen the remembered words gave me a much-needed shot in the soul. I knew then that I had at last bitten off a formidable hunk and, thank God, I still possessed all my natural teeth. I was in for some solid chewing.

The congregation found clothing and shoes for the children. At first three deacons volunteered to bring the children to church and almost at once the three resigned. Who could convey such a furious cargo to service? Each try was in each case decisive. So I volunteered. The boys twisted off a door handle, cracked a window, cut up a cushion, jumped up and down on the back seat and made it into a backyard swing.

Josephine became a nervous wreck trying to bring discipline to her untrained shock troops. Many church adults, as well, had a rather rough time trying to find the sacred rest in a shrine for which the gospel is famous. But who knows what infinite patience and whispering love can accomplish in this juvenile-delinquent world?

The very week after I prayed over a pail of potato peelings for the husband of the anguished woman, he got work! As he went by a construction yard, an old friend had called to him, and offered him a good job. So a second family started to attend divine service.

I paid many, many calls to the wobbling, creaking kitchen, and had many, many sessions with an alcoholic father, a weak-minded mother, and ten break-em-down-and-drag-em-out young'uns. For a year there were secret prayers and backstage conferences with the proper authorities.

Josephine may give us the final word, and when she does, she will probably say, "God did give me that dream. Didn't it come true?"

Portrait
of a Mother

WHEN I WAS a teen-aged boy, ranging the streets of Beverly, Massachusetts, I used to exclaim in moments of dejection and frustration, "Such is life without a wife and home without a baby!" I do not know who taught me the saying, but I learned later that life fills our empty phrases with rich and colorful meanings.

As a young pastor, I began to realize the kingdom, power and glory of the realm where Mother reigns solitary and supreme. My own wife was the first of four examples from which the full, composite portrait evolved.

For a third time during a month of suppers I had noticed my good wife's behavior at the table. I said nothing on any of the occasions, but after the third experience I went to my cluttered study and jotted down some of my thoughts. I will let the poem speak for itself:

Mother's Portion

Time and again I've watched my mother cut
Rye bread when there was not enough mince pie

To pass around.
Pa had his slice and Jane and Charles and I,
But Mother searched the shelves and silently
Ate what she found.
Sometimes a doughnut, cake from yesterday,
Or just a slice of bread, a pickle scrap
Left in the dill.
Ma ate her portion, quiet, thankfully,
Beaming the while she watched the rest of us
Having our fill.
Those days we did not seem to care or ask
Why mother always had to be the one
To sacrifice;
We never wondered why she searched the shelves
For crusts left over, missing, with a smile,
Things we thought nice—
If ever they were missed. Sometimes I think,
Now she has gone and on her grave the ferns
Nod restful, slow,
That no good thing in life can taste to us
Sweet as the bread our mother ate alone—
Long years ago.

The second part of the portrait was evoked by crisis, when my wife's mother lay at the point of death in Nova Scotia. The doctor urged a sister to summon the five children to their mother's bedside; four were in the United States. The elderly lady suffered with high blood pressure, arthritis, a weak heart and a huge kidney stone.

When my wife's sister urged us to go with other members of the family I felt an inner summons to pray. I recalled Jonah and his gourd: "And the Lord God prepared a gourd, and made it to come up over Jonah, that it might be a shadow over his head, to deliver him from his grief" (Jonah 4:6).

I thought of my cluster of Kentucky Wonders climbing over the tapering bean poles in a corner of the garden, and to this solitary greenery I retired. Alone, covered by the flickering shadows, I prayed to the same Lord God. While I prayed a Voice seemed to discuss matters with me.

"Do not go to Nova Scotia. Do not encourage your wife to go. I can hear prayer from here as well as from there. I can help her there. I am the Lord that healeth her.

"If you go, it will seem that you feel you can bring the required aid. You can't. Only I can sustain her in this crucial hour. If you stay here you will prove that you really count on *Me* to go for you and to do the required work."

Strange thoughts, indeed, that vibrated among wind, cloud and sunlight under the rustling stringbean leaves atop the green hill of old Westminster. Yet, did not the Eternal inform an ancient prophet: ". . . my thoughts are not your thoughts, neither are your ways my ways" (Isaiah 55:8)?

In the face of much coercion, my wife and I decided to remain in Connecticut. Many relatives thought we were peculiar, and our loyalties and devotion were questioned. But a greater mystery regarding the apparently dying woman can never be solved by human minds. Because of Mrs. Sullivan's blood pressure and heart weakness the physician could not operate to remove the stone that paralyzed the kidney. Therefore, when the suffering patient confessed relief in her back, the doctor was surprised.

In a week the pain subsided. The patient did not pass the stone, but X rays failed to find the least trace of it. The doctor scratched his head, saying, "I know it was there. Now, I know it isn't there. But it will come back." For seven years that stone has been numbered among the missing.

And soon my own mother in Beverly, Massachusetts, also suffered with an erratic heart, plus uncertain blood pressure and a terrible swollen right foot. A virus infection had reached a vital stage in the aggravated limb.

In honor of my parents' fifty-second wedding anniversary, my mother had summoned me from Connecticut to preach a sermon at the Gospel Mission Church. I arrived at two o'clock in the afternoon.

Mother sat in her rocking chair in the living room, with her right foot in a bowl of steaming water. She was pouring a solution of epsom salts from a small pitcher into the bowl. Her doctor had advised her to go to the hospital for treatment as soon as I arrived. Father was working in an oilcloth factory in Boston and would not be home until six.

Mother wrapped her foot in two towels and hobbled

to the car. As she limped into a back door of the hospital, she towered over the green slope like a queen on a throne. Her doctor had contacted his assistant, and he and two interns led my mother into a private room.

I waited a half-hour. Suddenly Mother strode out of the conference room leaning on a cane while she pushed her huge foot along the tiled floor. "No! I refuse to remain here!" She spoke decisively to the physician. Whenever I heard that firm, vigorous note in her voice, I trembled.

Two young interns bounced over to me. "Listen, Pastor. Your mother's got to stay here. We have a bed and room all fixed up. Her foot is dangerously infected, but we can't lance it now."

"Why not?"

"Her heart. It's pounding like a triphammer. We want to put her to bed, calm her nerves, administer sedatives. Tomorrow morning she will be right for the operation."

Mother's sharp ears caught the drift of conversation and she hobbled over to us.

"Philip!" she trumpeted. "You know this is my wedding anniversary. You know how I've waited for and counted on that anniversary sermon."

She faced the young interns with her eyes flaming and cheeks flushed, "My son has driven one hundred and twenty miles to preach a sermon tonight—for Victor and me! And I shall be there to hear it!"

The approaching doctor, the staggered interns surrounded me. "You have seen your mother's foot, you . . ."

"Philip, take me home!"

Mother pushed the toweled, heavy foot toward a sunny hospital door. An orderly grabbed me by the elbow and I whirled at him.

"Do you think *anybody* can stop my mother when she's made up her mind?" I asked.

"But, Pastor, really. . . ."

"Please get out of my way!" Mother commanded an orderly as though he were a stubborn boy and with her cane she tapped his elbow.

Doctors, orderlies, nurses stared, speechless, as my mother burst through the swinging doors, out into a great pool of sunlight. "I wouldn't be checked into the hospital without your father's permission, anyway," she notified me as I drove her home. "I never make an important decision without consulting Victor."

Mother bathed her foot at home until meeting time and then attended the advertised service. In the front seat she faced the pulpit, her throbbing, angry leg arranged on a chair to ameliorate the pain. After services, she and my father played their guitars and sang an old-time favorite. The worshiping congregation were enthralled by the power and deathlessness of the wedding spirit.

Mother returned home to bury the fiercely painful foot in fresh applications of hot epsom salts. "I am resolved to go to the hospital. Victor has approved." And so I left her and proceeded upstairs to bed.

In the morning I spied mother again in the rocking chair. The right foot was still in steaming water. "Did you sleep at all?" I inquired, timidly.

"Listen, Son. You are a preacher, aren't you?"

"I hope I am."

"Didn't you pray for me last night?"

"Why, yes."

"Didn't you ask God to take care of this foot?"

"Yes, I did."

"Well, He did! God lanced it—in the night, while I slept. It ruined the sheets and the mattress, I think, but I don't care. I feel much better this morning. God is a very wise Surgeon, Son. You must trust Him more."

Thrilled by Mother's victory of faith I returned to Canterbury to listen to an even more amazing narrative. It became the fourth part of a portrait of mother love.

My wife, my children and I paid a friendly call on a family down the West Bend Road. From a friendly farmwoman, her jovial husband and their pretty, vivacious daughter, we heard an unforgettable story of love.

"Can I see my baby?" the happy new mother asked.

When the little bundle was nestled in her arms and she moved the fold of cloth to look upon his tiny face, she gasped. The doctor turned quickly and looked out the tall hospital windows. The baby boy had been born without ears.

Time proved that the boy's hearing was perfect. Only his appearance was marred. When he rushed home from school one day and flung himself into his mother's arms, she sighed, knowing that his life would be a succession of tragedies.

"I got—got into a fight—I didn't mean to!" He blurted out. "A boy—a big boy called me a—a freak!"

The boy grew up to be handsome, except for his disfigurement. He was a favorite with his fellow students and might have been elected class president but—for that. He developed poetic gifts and a talent for literature and music.

"But you must mingle with other people." His mother reproved him for his introverted habits. The boy's father had a session with the family physician to find out whether anything could be done.

"I believe I could graft on a pair of outer ears, if they could be obtained," the doctor decided. So a search was begun for a person who would make such a sacrifice for a young man with the promise of a brilliant future. The search dragged wearily over two discouraging years. Then, one day, the father said, "You are going to the hospital, Son. Mother and I have found someone who is willing to give you a pair of ears. But the person's name is to be a deep secret."

The boy trembled and rushed into his father's arms. "Oh, Father! Oh, Father!" was all he could say.

The operation was a success and a new person emerged from the surgical ward. The boy's talents blossomed into genius, and school and college became a series of stirring victories. Later he married a beautiful, accomplished woman, and they had children. He entered the diplomatic service and rose to a top position.

"I must know," he kept urging his father. "I must know who gave up so much for me. I could never do enough for that person."

"I do not believe you could," agreed the solemn parent. "But the arrangement was that you should not be told."

The years kept their profound secret until the son stood with his grim father at his mother's casket. Slowly, tenderly, the father moved close to the casket, stretched forth a hand and raised the woman's thick, reddish-brown hair to reveal that she had no ears.

"Mother was glad she had never cut her hair," he whispered hoarsely. "Nobody would ever suspect, she told me. She could easily hide her misfortune." His eyes were bright prisms as he said gently, "And we never thought she was less beautiful, did we?"

Flight into Shadows

ONE DAY A NEIGHBOR on Tatnic Hill Road asked whether I had ever called on the Baptist minister. "Baptist minister?" I exclaimed. "Is there a man of the cloth on one of these farms?"

"They say one lives in the old Ellis place."

I asked all my friends who lived on the twisting road, but not one of them could add a salt-pinch of information to the tiny morsel I had. Well, the only way to find out something is—to find out. So I continued to drive along the road, around dizzy curves and up surprising grades. Sometimes the road became a mere scrap as it squeezed between tremendous barns.

Up on a gray rock ledge I saw a sprawling gray farmhouse in dire need of paint, fore and aft, up and down. The yard was a squat, somber area of rock and dirt. A half-dozen scraggly, wind-torn trees stood about the building like great, gray ghosts or the masts of landlocked ships.

"Nobody lives here," I said to myself as I knocked on a faded, rain-warped front door. The curtains were drawn and the blinds closed, yet I thought I saw a yellow glow behind one window. I struggled along a weed-choked path, where burrs clung to my best pants and dug into my ankles. I pounded lustily on the back door and finally tried a small side door.

At my third port of call I heard a distant footfall, a fussing with an unseen latch, and a rustling at the outer door. A bolt slipped free and the door opened a crack.

"What . . . do . . . you . . . want?"

"I am the preacher on the hill, making pastoral calls," I answered. "I heard that a Baptist minister lives here."

"You . . . are . . . pastor?" The door creaked open another inch.

"Yes, and I thought I might explore the possibilities for ministerial fellowship."

"You . . . come . . . to say . . . good-day?"

"That's all."

The door opened a few more inches. I stared, gulped, not knowing whether I looked upon an old man or a little old woman. A checkered scarf was wound tightly about the head and held to the throat by one hand. A pair of small, sepia-brown eyes seemed to look inward rather than out. The pale, thin face was wrinkled and leathery. Black trousers defined the stranger as a man.

"Are you a minister?" I inquired.

"Ssh! Come in," he whispered. "Step inside."

I entered a small space, between a woodshed and a kitchen. The man snapped on a mild electric bulb and offered me a trembling hand.

"Yes, I am a Baptist pastor—refugee from Estonia."

"Your name?" Stealthily he told me. I must not dare to divulge it, or my friend would perish in the blaze of the publicity like a flower already withering in the sun.

"You are married?" I asked.

He glanced about cautiously before he replied, "Yes, I have wife—sick. She is in bed."

"And children?"

Again the apprehensive shudder. "Boy in Jersey and girl in Ohio."

"You live here? Only you and your wife?"

"That is right."

"I had no idea. I have passed this house a dozen times."

"We are quiet people," he whispered. "We are people of the shadows. We move in them, we prefer them. We shall finish our earthly pilgrimage in them. We dwell all the time under the shadow of the Almighty. He has put us there—we must stay there."

"It's hard to supply a pulpit in the country," I said. "Perhaps you would preach for me some Sabbath."

"That I could not do." The man began to tremble and his teeth chattered. A cloud of fears engulfed his pallid face. "You must not ask me, brother. I am here in this quiet place. I must remain in God's shadows."

"How do you live?"

"My son brings me money occasionally, and my daughter, too. A few Estonian people come here one night a month. We have a meeting—they give me a collection. But, brother, please do not mention meeting." A thin hand fussed with my right wrist. "You will let us be quiet here . . . and . . . forgotten?"

I did not reveal my thoughts to a brother pastor.

"It was good to have these words, brother. My wife may need me, so excuse me, please."

The outer door groaned again and I stepped into the yard. The instant I cleared the threshhold the door closed. The bolt sounded like the crack of doom.

At last I had found another pastor in the hard-pressed old township. I wondered whether we would have good fellowship.

As I called again and again at the gray haunt in the shadows, the old house resembled more and more the hull of a derelict ship. The windows were like port holes against wind, water and sky. There was no entrance fore or aft—only a gangplank thrust into the side where the woodbox met the galley. The noiseless shadow-shapes that came and went seemed to be two ghosts that haunted a ship cast high and dry on a rocky ledge.

More than once the plaintive lines of Omar Khayyam came to me as I entered and departed the gangway of the spectral hull:

> We are no other than a moving row
> Of visionary Shapes that come and go
>   Round with this Sun-illumin'd Lantern held
> In Midnight by the Master of the Show. . . .

174

Once I thought I caught a glimpse of the pastor's wife behind a curtained window, and once, I think, I heard her voice from behind a locked door; I can't be sure. I never got beyond the kitchen door. The open space between cordwood and kitchen was all that was granted me for a vantage point.

"You must go out sometime," I urged the quiet pastor one day. "How can you or your wife be healthy when you are shut in like this? We are going to have a fellowship supper at the church—"

"No, no!" he interrupted with unusual spirit. "We must not go."

In his excitement he opened the door to the interior of the house. A bitter, nauseous odor rose up from the hidden places to stagger me.

"Brother, brother," he whispered, "I will tell you why God has put us in the shadows."

"For years I was Protestant pastor, Baptist pastor in Estonia. I had fine church, good people, in border town. One night Russian regiment came into town. This was before Bolshevik rev-o-lu-tion." I noted the way he looked as he spoke the word, as though it were something to flee. Glowing coals shone in his introvert eyes and a vibrant deeper tone crept into his modulated voice. As his hand began to move, his pulpit form trembled into being!

"Russian regiment go on spree. Men got drunk, soldiers start to shoot up town. I have great friend, merchant, deacon. He hear commotion and rush out into streets to scold scoldiers. Someone shot him dead—shot him like dog in the streets."

"His wife hurry to me. She plead with me to go see if he is really dead. I go—and find deacon in blood on street. I go to Russian captain and complain." The narrator was painting the scene with an unexpected flow of passion.

"Russian captain glare at me, spit on me. 'Hah, you priest! I not like priest! You come to make trouble! Tomorrow be maybe your turn!' He knocked me down, then drew a sword and cut hole in the air. He looked down, grinned. I never forget grin, never."

My friend must have been a forceful preacher. His words had caught me in their spell. He continued. "I hurry home. Told Mamma to get up, dress children. At midnight we flee, leave church, home, everything. We reach German border; see church and state official. We come to this country." He panted like an animal that had been tracked down, worn out. His slight body seemed ready to collapse under the impact of revelation.

"But you are safe here," I encouraged.

"I am not sure. That Russian captain, way he speak, he grin. His people in power over there . . . now. He threaten to kill me. Brother, you know now why God hide us away under His shadow?"

What could I do but lay hold of a trembling hand? I tried to say words of faith and courage that in such an hour one cannot say fittingly.

The revelation had been too significant, too perilous. A month later when I called on Tatnic Hill Road I knocked on the side door. There was no response.

I never learned anything more about the Baptist pastor. I sometimes wonder where he is. In what new haunt of silence and shadow does he hide? How can he care for a sick wife? Is he still afraid he will lose a son, a daughter? There are many such questions to which a terribly preoccupied world turns a deaf ear.

Should I, by the remotest possibility, chance upon him again, I shall suggest that he seek solace and comfort in a prayer he may not know. I shall share it with him—if we ever meet:

> O Lord, support us all the day long of this troublous life, until the shadows lengthen, and the evening comes, and the busy world is hushed, and the fever of life is over, and our work is done. Then of Thy mercy grant us a safe lodging, and a holy rest, and peace at the last; through Jesus Christ our Lord. Amen.

An Old Woman's
Angel-Birds

A COUNTRY PASTOR must be braced for any emergency. I often ponder a Bible admonition: "Boast not thyself of to morrow; for thou knowest not what a day may bring forth" (Proverbs 27:1). A day may bring a plague of flies; it may drive a mad dog to the church lawn; or spill a gala wedding party in the manse driveway; it may whirl a preacher out upon the midnight roads seeking the lost; it may surround him with a flock of sheep. One morning two donkeys hoof-marked our tender new lawn. They brayed, kicked heels and turf into the air, almost scaring my wife out of her wits. While we visited the sick or cheered the discouraged, a stray cow, more than once, has invaded our premises and we returned to a mighty sick-looking garden.

And a pastor may have no end of troubles with a fugitive handful of birds! Light, airy wings that fly over a church roof can also strike panic in some good hearts and become the wings of irrevocable Destiny.

I thought everything possible had happened to me until one day a woefully thin spinster of some seventy years tramped with a cane into an empty church; empty, that is, except for me.

Looking at her, I thought of the New Hampshire farmer who decided to chisel a religious line on his departed wife's gravestone. One line appealed to him, "O Lord, she was Thine." But his length of stone ran out and so the inscription read: "O Lord, she was Thin."

My visitor was a good soul, I learned, who lived alone except for her cats, plants and birds. Orioles, bluebirds, scarlet tanagers, robins—these were her angels of the upper air. Starlings were the black-winged evil spirits of the universe.

"Pastor Cleveland!" she called in sharp, trumpet tones. "Are you h-e-r-e?"

I had been sitting in a pulpit chair, enjoying a meditative hour. The sacred desk had sheltered me. I stood.

"Gracious me!" she exclaimed, a bit wobbly for an instant. "Gracious me! Never scare a lady like that, just bobbing up out of nowhere! Wait a moment till I catch my breath."

She caught it and continued. "You've got to do something—something drastic—about your birds. They are becoming a public nuisance!"

"What do I have," I stuttered, "that is becoming a public nuisance?"

180

"Your birds, your miserable starlings, Pastor Cleveland!"

"M-m-my miserable starlings?" I stammered. "W-w-what is this all about?"

"You stand there and say you don't know?"

"Of course I don't know."

"You don't know what is going on around your own church?" The cane thumped the church floor, her thin, wrinkled face flushed. Her clipped words suggested a sharp pair of shears.

"I wish you would speak plainly," I suggested.

"Haven't you seen those *thieves, robbers, villains* around the church?" she exploded. "Around the belfry, I mean—those wretched starlings?"

"Yes, I've seen them. What about them?"

"What about them?" she whirled. "I'll tell you! They're *robbers, villains!* I can't feed my angel-birds lately on account of your miserable villains! I throw out crumbs for *my* birds and *your* birds tear out of the belfry and gobble up every single bit before my birds can get any. Now my birds won't come into my yard."

"My birds?" I objected. "I cannot say that they are *my* birds." I tried to pour healing oil upon the troubled waters of the sanctuary.

"Then whose are they?"

She raised a hand to drive a hairpin or two into her luxuriant puffs of iron-gray hair. Oodles of them, clinging to her head, were being shaken loose by her vigor.

"Whose belfry do they live in, just waiting for me to feed my birds before they darken the skies? If they aren't yours, Pastor Cleveland, pray tell me whose birds they are?"

"They are God's."

"You know better than that. If not, you are very stupid."

"You think they—"

She brooked no interruption, but continued with increased tempo. "And I want this villainy stopped! Stopped at once! Do you hear me?"

"How can I stop the starlings?"

"Get a shotgun! Shoot them!"

"Thou shalt not kill."

"Good riddance to bad rubbish!"

"I'm not a good shot."

"Hire someone who is! Hire a carpenter, let him stretch a heavy wire netting around the belfry so the birds can't hide in the shadows!"

"Will you pay the bill?"

"Gracious me! Most certainly not! This isn't my church. It's up to you to confine your own criminals!"

"The church hasn't the proper funds at present to build a scaffolding and work on the belfry."

"You'll do something or I'll have the law on you!"

"You really don't mean that."

"Don't I? You think that because I'm a poor, defenseless old lady you can take advantage of me and plunder

my property and drive all my angels away?" Her loud,
explosive words, stabbed with hair-pin exclamations,
ended in a sudden rush of tears. She turned and thumped
from the sanctuary, crying, "You will hear from me
again if this villainy isn't attended to."

I talked to the good Lord about my remarkable problem of church discipline, because only heaven guesses
the hardships and difficulties of a rural parish. Starlings
in the belfry!

I certainly did hear again from the aggrieved neighbor.
A typewritten letter ordered me to hasten and find a solution to the crime. I still have that letter in my own old
curiosity shop. Only the bleak starling shadows glistened
in the sunlight among birch, elm, maple and oak trees.
And who could feel anger against the bereaved old
woman who hoped each dawn that her angelic creatures
would return.

It is impossible to trace the hidden courses of events.
I only know that New England suffered its most prolonged summer drought in fifty years. The earth was
parched and burned. Not only orioles, bluejays and
robins winged to wetter states, but my starlings, too,
rushed off to happier hunting grounds. In the next spring
a neighbor's flowery yard awoke once more to bursts of
birdsong, and the dear lady heats again for me the cere-
monial pot of tea.

Manni's New World

I HAD COMPLETED this book when my wife asked: "Aren't you going to tell the story of Manni?" And, I thought again of our Jewish friend, Emanuel.

I remembered an April downpour, the rutted, flooded rural roads and an afternoon jaunt. I had heard about two twelve-year-old boys who attended the school but not the church, and my search for those stray lambs led me to their shepherd.

By arrangement with the boys I followed the yellow school bus for two miles into South Canterbury, to the old Quinebaug River pines. The two lads jumped into my car when the bus stopped and directed me along a slimy, rain-filled country road. Our journey ended in a kitchen where two men played cards on a substantial table.

"These boys ought to go to church," I prompted, after exchanging introductions.

"They are state wards. We are taking care of them for the time being," the shorter man, a Dutchman, explained.

"They ought to be in church. And you, too, should attend services," I informed him. I turned to the second man. "You, sir, would also be welcome."

"You think . . . a Jew . . . would be welcome in your church?" he returned. Under the yellow kitchen bulb his head looked very large. Tufts of gray-white hair fringed a bald crown. His features were heavy; his deep-set brown eyes smouldered like banked fires.

He was overweight, all of him, with the torso of a giant and the arms and legs of a mortal. His voice was as small as his body was large. It suggested a Chopin sonata —delicate, tuneful, appealing. In all, he bore a remarkable resemblance to William Jennings Bryan. "Your people do not always welcome my people in their midst. We are not accepted in New England," he said.

"You'd be accepted on the hill," I assured him. "In fact, I'd be honored, sir, to have you in my congregation some Sabbath. You are a flesh and blood brother to the most wonderful Person who ever lived. He came forth from the rugged loins of your people. He was child of Abraham, Moses, David. Our church can never pay its debt to your people for their gift to us."

Manni took my measure the way a tailor might have taken it. His sheltered eyes seemed to step out from beneath shaggy roofs in order to appraise me. "You do not believe in pogroms—persecutions?" he inquired. "You do not despise my people?"

"My Teacher said we should love one another."

"Yes," he owned, speaking with more vigor. "I have always wondered why your people preach love, while they despise the kith and kin of the Man who proclaimed love. They have always seemed insincere to me." Manni proceeded to recite incidents of persecution against Jews in my own New England.

I tried to sum up my thoughts. "All I can say is that I am going back to the church to polish an old Yankee pew for you."

My challenge was accepted and on the following Lord's day Manni sat in an old church that had been raised in 1770 on high Westminster Hill. Seated with him were a man, a woman and two youngsters. The woman was the Dutchman's wife, a registered nurse, who was helping Manni to convalesce after a serious illness.

After the service a dozen members of the congregation shook Manni's hand vigorously and invited him to come again. He availed himself of every possible opportunity to accept. Though he was a widower with married children, he enjoyed the simple life, and allowed a relative to manage his business affairs.

One Sunday after services he came for dinner at the manse. When I realized we were serving pork and beans for the table, I had the jitters. To a strict Israelite pork is a forbidden meat. As my wife prepared dinner I offered apologies in the living room. "Manni, our brains aren't percolating today. I forgot to consider your customs. My wife is warming up pork and beans, and you of course do not eat pork."

He bent close to me, reached for one of my hands, and rubbed it gently as he looked at my fingers.

"Is the dinner coming to me from your hand?"

"Yes, Manni, such as it is. I am sorry, but—"

He interrupted with a graceful smile. "Is it coming from your hand?"

"Why, yes."

"Could the meat be *pig*, if it is coming from *your* hand? How could it?" Never has anyone blended more haunting music with the human voice, or thrust so meaningful a smile into a country pastor's home.

On my wife's birthday Manni drove his car to our back door and opened the trunk. Gifts of flowers, a cut-glass pitcher and glasses, silverware and candy poured from the shining vault into our kitchen. Coming to the door like an unseasonal Santa, he called, "Angel," a name he had given my wife. "These are for you. Preacher's wives do not receive proper consideration from a busy world. I hope you are pleased, Angel."

She was speechless, utterly overwhelmed by the deluge of delights and delicacies.

"On my recent Florida trip," Manni informed us, "I spoke of your church as my church. I told my rabbi that I would give half of my donation to Westminster Church. He thinks I'm losing my mind. Do you think I'm in my dotage, Angel?"

"The great Teacher challenged us to be more simple and childlike," my wife replied.

"You always say the right things," he said.

The Dutchman once hinted that an anonymous benefactor was paying some of the church's bills for lumber, nails and other materials as our damaged steeple rose proudly back into the heavens. We tried but could not solve the mystery.

And then Manni's nurse called to tell us that he was very ill in the hospital. When we arrived, his brother was in the room talking to him. One of Manni's hands reached for Angel's gentle fingers, while the other seized upon my rough hands.

"So glad you have come," he said, with a kindly smile. To his brother he announced, "These are the people I told you about."

As the four of us bowed our heads, I asked the great, all-wise Father to take very special care of Manni, to ease the pain, to give His beloved one sleep, to cheer him with the knowledge of the vast, wonderful love that surrounded him day and night. Before leaving the room I said to him, "Sholom aleichem."

He answered so beautifully, "Aleichem sholom."

"Peace be unto you"—"And peace unto you likewise" —With those words the Master had greeted His disciples in the fargone, marvelous days.

A week later Manni closed his weary, lonely eyes. His last words were about his dear, departed wife and the mercy of Elohim over all his days. It had been his request that a country minister should give the funeral oration over his grave at the Beth Israel cemetery in Norwich, and the Jewish authorities gave me a special dispensation. I made an honest attempt to pay fitting tribute to a most generous man.

Manni had found his final Year of Jubilee in rural

Canterbury. He called upon the dairymen, the chicken and vegetable farmers. His neighbors thought the world of him, and he drove often to a distant city to buy them their favorite delicacies. The church doors ushered him into a new, thrilling world where he built friendships with Finns, Russians, Germans, and the precise, matter-of-fact Yankees. For a short time he lived the abundant life which the Shepherd of His sheep had pledged His people so very long ago.

His last visit to the church was unexpected. I thought he had gone to New London, but just before the sermon he took a seat in the half-way pew that suited him.

I had selected for my sermon the theme of Christ before Pilate. The brutal trial of the Lord involved the perfidy of the Jewish leaders, the hatred of the high priest and the treachery of the Jewish temple.

Should I preach that sermon or shift to another theme? I decided to proceed according to plan.

The moment the benediction was concluded I hurried down the aisle to him. My nervous right hand was caught in a heavy, soothing palm. Manni's full-moon face beamed and his sonorous voice was reassuring.

"Reverend, your sermons are getting better all the time."

I wonder, sometimes, if he did not die a Christian, after all!

Epilogue

THE BUILDER

The Child of Nazareth, He loved to build
Things as a Boy; His hands oft gathered wood
Along the roads and with a knife carved lines
Of simple beauty there—the best He could.

In later years, a stalwart Youth, His hands
Sure with the saw and firm as hardened will
Would build a chair, a door, a peasant's tool,
In Joseph's busy shop high on the hill.

And when He built a house, the eaves were found
Straight as a plumb-line; every oxgoad sent
Forth to the fields from His stout arm was strong;
No wall He ever sold was warped or bent.

And He built bodies as He built a home—
Straight and secure; His hands reached out to all
Who called His name; the beggar's twisted frame
Beneath His hands reared like a finished wall.

And so with souls—His lips would move and mend
Each broken suppliant with faith and love;
Great healing surged from His clear, sinless eyes
And truth rang in His voice from God above.

God, send Your Carpenter down from the height—
Man's world is full of broken things tonight!